Invest & Insure

by
J. TRIP

2017

Invest and Insure
First Edition 2017

by
J. TRIP

Kapil Publishers
23440 Sycamore Creek Avenue
Murrieta, CA 92562, USA
Phone : 404-717-3154
E-Mail : jayasri.misra@gmail.com
ISBN: 978-0-9993152-1-7

****

Printer :
BookLogix, Alpharetta, USA

****

Printing, Design & Type Setting
Manoj Agrawal, Raipur Chhattishgarh, INDIA
Mobile : +919826910357, +919300610357
E-Mail : mkagrawalryp@gmail.com

****

Front Cover :
Elephant and Blind Men
Michele Bury, Gautam Misra, and Anamika Misra

Dedicated

to...

the people, clients and prospects, includes, suspects,
of Atlanta and elsewhere who by their
participation helped me learn the
business of Financial Planning, Insurance,
Real Estate, Mortgage and Investments
for the last 30 years
and
eventually accomplish my transition out
of Teaching and Research
in Biology, Microbiology, Genetics,
and Recombinant DNA Technology.

Disclaimer

The comments and advise in this book are for information
purposes only. Competent Accountant, Attorney, Stock
Broker, Realtor, Lender, Insurance Agent and others must be
consulted to implement the ideas mentioned in these articles.

Author, Invest & Insure.

Introduction

The name of the book, Invest & Insure, is based on the name of our business, Invest & Insure.

Working with several insurance and investment companies between 1985-1992, I felt the need of my own business entity, for independence and flexibility, as well as better client service and higher value proposition. Hence we formed, Invest & Insure Enterprises in 1991 and started offering insurance and investment services as independent brokers. We announced our firm to be called, 'Insurance and Investment Services'. Since i left working with a particular firm, the source of prospects and clients slowly dried up. I had to go to numerous networking events, join the lead clubs, put advertisements to generate a stream of prospects and clients, since none of the captive companies will provide any help, in bringing new prospects.

In one of the networking meetings, where you put your name on an adhesive slip and paste it to your shirt or jacket for name recognition, the name slip was too small, and i could not fit the entire, Insurance and Investment Services, on it, hence shortened the name to 'Invest & Insure', and started using the phrase on our stationary and business cards.

Eventually, this smaller name got registered with authorities. Then comes the story of writing the book. I had written several books in biology. I also used to write articles on taxation, insurance, investments, real estate and mortgage, since i considered them complimentary to each other. Kailash Khandelwal was publishing a monthly magazine, Atlanta Dunia, in our city (Johns Creek, GA) for several years and asked me to write a column for it called, Biz Buzz, where i regularly contributed, every month, an article for Atlanta Dunia for 2-3 years. Most of the articles have been taken from this Magazine. Hence they are short, do not provide much details, but entice people / readers to look for further information, still providing basic idea of a particular topic, which we come across, very often in our financial dealings.

I have considered Financial Planning, as an Art, rather than a Science, and believe that each Planner follows a unique course that he/she finds appropriate for a particular client, and a specific situation. Instead of being specialized with one narrow area, I have practiced a broad view of the subject of insurance, providing plans for property and casualty (cars, homes, boat, motorcycles, buildings, umbrella, liability, malpractice, workers compensation, business insurance etc), accident and sickness (medical, dental, vision, disability, critical care, long term care etc), Life and Disability Insurance, Education and Retirement Funding, through several insurers and investment firms. I generally try to provide a comprehensive and holistic approach to the clients' problems.

I combine these with Tax situations and Real Estate needs, thus providing several kinds of services, and try to keep my clients in Financial Balance.

Hence the cover of the book explains the Elephant examined by Blind Men, who describe a narrow aspect of their experience and disagree in their approaches, while i like to address several fields together.

Hope this makes some sense, and provides enough competent service in the areas of Planning and Financial Risk Management.

Acknowledgements

Manoj Agrawal, Raipur, India has been a great help in composing and preparing the book for the press.

Nisha and Kailash Khandelwal of Atlanta Dunia Johns Creek, GA allowed the use of previously published articles from his magazine.

Several other magazines freely allowed to use my previously published pieces in their publications. I am indebted to all of them.

Bijay Choudhary and Brajmohan Mishra of Darbhanga, Bihar, India was instrumental in arranging finances for the expenses incurred in India, at a short notice.

There have been numerous other friends, members of my extended family, associates and institutions that made it possible to complete this work and bring it to fruition. They all have been very kind to me, and I salute, them all.

Many sources may not have been identified properly. Like the talks I heard at NAIFA, National Association of Insurance and Financial Advisors, MDRT, Million Dollar Round Table, Insurance Company Conventions over the years; Byline Article from Insurers, SFSP, Society for Financial Service Professionals, Life Leaders Groups, etc, all contributed to my ideas mentioned here.

CONTENTS

	Chapters	**Page**

(1)

Annuities

'What should I do with my Money ?

The answer, not exactly, but a probing question to determine the right answer, was …'What do you want your money to do while you are alive, and what do you want it to do, after you die ? Asked the financial advisor.

Here is what I want, said the money man, the investor.

I want a guaranteed pay check every month for the rest of my life. And when I die, I want my wife to get the same check, every month for the rest of her life. When she dies, we want our son to get that same check for the rest of his life. And when he dies, his wife, our daughter-in-law, should get the same check for her life.

And finally, when his wife dies, we want our grand-daughter to get the same check for the rest of her life. That is what I want.

All this can be achieved through a well crafted Annuity. Insurance companies are the only institutions that can use Mortality Credits and design a scheme, Retirement Income Annuity, that can last for generations, with guaranteed and predictable income.

Annuities are reverse of Life Insurance. In life insurance you pay smaller amounts in premiums, and expect a big pay out, a lump sum of money, when you die or retire. In annuities you pay a big lump sum of money, up front, say the accumulated value of a retirement plan or the life time of savings, and receive a regular, monthly income for ever, on guaranteed basis.

(9)

(2)

Asset Allocation

Stock market has been touted as the best place to invest money for a long term. However, for the last decade this has not proved to be so. But what else has done better ? Real Estate, Precious metals and the rest ? Modest risk free gains are still available in several other places, but stock market remains a darling of the people. Hence risk management, rebalancing of portfolio at regular intervals, asset allocation and prudent selection of a mix of various kinds of investments is necessary for a steady growth, and for the protection from big losses.

Many a times just one target date fund, and just one diversified ETF can do all the trick, without ever lifting a finger for decent performance of portfolio, if one can show some patience and not fall into the trap of frequent buying and selling.

For younger people almost 90% of portfolio should be in stocks for growth, it is high risk, high return account since the time to recoup any losses is plenty. For older people close to retirement, the mix of stocks and bonds becomes 50-50, during the period 5 years prior to and 5 years after retirement. One has to sacrifice the high return of stocks for the safety of bonds, as there is not enough time left to handle any set backs and reversals in the market. However, many a times bonds may be more volatile than stocks due to interest rate fluctuation. Even at ages past 90, one still needs some stocks in the portfolio to act as kicker and generate decent returns.

One should take into account a diversified portfolio in various asset classes and sectors for a balanced performance.

(3)

Balance Sheet

Business Owners often deal with 'Assets, Liabilities, and Net Worth'. In addition, they always think of 'Gross Income, Net Income, and Cash Flow'. The personal as well as business situations, very soon create a 'Financial World' which is complex, haphazard and difficult to manage. Running a business successfully requires numerous responsibilities to tackle. Often the business and personal matters get intertwined in such a way that, it becomes difficult to separate them, and it is hard to follow the golden rule, 'no commingling of personal and business assets'.

A successful business requires a personal retirement planning for owner(s) and key employees, good mortgage and loan selection, cash flow and protection plans, in place for handling contingencies and risks of various kinds. It becomes difficult, many a times, to balance the important business focus, with personal financial opportunities. The four important financial domains — protection, assets, liabilities, and cash flow — across the business and personal domains, become a complex maze, which become increasingly difficult to handle with time.

A business owner generally contracts with a number of firms to provide for personal and employee needs, most of which remain isolated in reporting. Different firms provide, property and casualty insurance, retirement plans, personal life-disability insurance etc. In addition, different people may be handling the employee benefits plans, like medical, dental, vision, short- and long-term disability, long term care and life and accident insurances. The task of coordinating this array of information and its proper administration is left to the single individual who owns a small business or a so called, Human Resource Officer.

An IT-based program to integrate all business and personal data, to store them and to retrieve them whenever needed, in a manageably way, is achieved by a Balance Sheet approach, for both personal and business needs, integrated into a common platform. This service is available free of cost, just for the asking.

Banking

Bankers are considered rich and powerful. We all bank, since we can not hold funds for long and safely under the mattress, and inside the pillow.

There are international banks, money center banks, regional banks and local banks.

Citicorp extends into numerous countries, Bank of America and Wachovia are the largest US Banks. BBT and Regions Financial are regional banks. Numerous local banks exist in every city, and on every street corner. Over half a dozen Indians own their banks in the greater Atlanta area and elsewhere.

Writing about banks is a huge task, however, I will confine to the three following aspects of banking :

1. Where and how to bank : where to keep your funds invested for short durations, and for long haul,

2. How to secure loans for personal and business needs from a bank or financial institution, and

3. How to start a bank of your own.

Bank Where : Banks are necessary evils. One puts funds in a local bank for ease of transaction, as the old barter system has gradually vanished. But banks offer you 0.2-0.5% return on your deposits, and charge you 5-9% on lending the same funds to you. The spread between these two numbers makes banks rich. Banks also issue credit cards and charge huge interest, say 10-15% or more for allowing you quick credit. Thus all of the deposits in savings, checking, money market, CDs (Certificate of deposit should be called Certificate of Depreciation/Despair), make sure you loose your buying power by 3-5% each year, considering the taxes you pay on interest/ dividends, and the inflation that makes things more and more expensive over the time. All this is, of course, federally guaranteed, under FDIC. The barter system evolved into collecting funds in the mattress and finally into banking for ease and safety. But smart banking, now available so freely, generates 5-6% tax-free interest at numerous financial institutions.

Securing Loans : For securing loan/mortage for buying property (home, car, buildings and other stuff) or for conducting business, one again has to work with banks. Banks have a large pool of money at their disposal, and, thus have a large control on our financial affairs. The sub-prime mess, and the turmoil in financial markets has lately proved, how ill-managed the banks are. And how greedy and irrational the banks can be, by awarding loans to unqualified borrowers, in the hope of getting outrageous returns on their investments. With minor adjustments in ones borrowing habits, one can create a stream of overdraft protection, and can manage borrowing and banking on their own and be less dependent on the financial institutions.

Own Bank : In spite of all its negative connotations, the lucrative banking business has attracted a host of people. If seven to ten people get together, collect $25,000 or so each, hire an attomey, and accountant, and a banking expert, they should succeed in less than a year, obtaining a charter to establish a bank of their own.

The board of directors, the original 7/10 people, then hire an expert as CEO to run the bank in a building, or a permanent physical location. The process is cumbersome, needs proper planning, hard work and commitment from members to go through the arduous steps. Just a group of 3/5 enthusiastic people, with the support of 7/10 silent investors/partners, could establish a bank by approaching the banking-commission. The initial members can sell their shares for a quick profit, buy more (other's) shares. It takes normally 2/3 years to make a bank profitable and eventually helps project an image of success, pride and financial freedom, for those who like to proceed with caution.

(5)

Business Succession

How many small businesses can eventually rise to the level of big corporations like IBM, Microsoft or Coca Cola? Very, very few. Since very few people, who begin as mon-and-pop operations, in a basement or a garage or in a dingy, dark office with just one employee, are as smart, and can dream as big, as the founders or these famous corporations did. Once you dream big, then comes the numerous steps of hard work, smarts and planning. US has millions of small businesses that are said to be the back bone of our economy, and they form the largest number of employers of people. Numerous businesses open their doors everyday, while many others shut theirs' all the time.

Even the most successful small businesses do not survive after second or third generation of their founders.

Growing into a large corporation is rare, but putting up plans to make a business survive even for a few generations is not easy. Let us discuss the measures to help Business Continuation or Succession, for small businesses, beyond the life and time of their founders, so that future generations and future owners may not have to invent the wheel again and again.

Protecting a business in the event of an untimely death and / or disability of a major shareholder or key owner, should be among the first concerns of any company. Proper planning for contingencies for the financial security of the business ensures future survival of the business. Corporations, Partnerships, limited Liability Companies, Sole Proprietorships all need to address Business Successions ASAP, as soon as possible.

The first step should be contact the Advisors to your (own)

business. The attorney, the accountant and Financial Planner can help develop succession strategies. The kind of business entity is important. C-, S-, LL- corporations, are required for perpetual existence of the business. Assemble your most competent (key employees) staff and any family memeber who will be responsible to run the business in your absence or when the owner/founder is not available, due to death, sickness or retirement.

Selling the business to a partner or associate or transferring the ownership to a family member, has to be done very carefully. Deciding Succession depends upon the competence, interest and expected compensation of/to the Successor.

Prior to making any decision the business needs to be valued of its worth. Multiple factors affect the value of a business and its future worth to a buyer and/or an inheritor. Tax and business valuation, as well as future projections are complex matters and further insight from the Advisor(s) is/are required. A buy-sell agreement between partners/owners is like a Will for the business, which can be accomplished with a Cross-purchase-, redemption- or entity agreement. A wait-and-see clause can also be added. Restricting the future ownership, minimization of taxes, and limit the disruption of the business should be the main concern in any such arrangement.

Strategies for estate conservation, setting up trusts, ILIT (irrevocable life insurance trust). and gifting to charity and family (heirs) can be accomplished with a cross- or entity-purchase agreements, and stock redemption plans. A regular review of the plans and keeping them current with tax and inheritance laws should also be a part of the overall planning so that the Succession may continue, at ease, in both favorable and difficult times/circumstances.

Casino-USA

Why do people feel mistreated by wall street, big banks, large corporations, the government and politicians? Why are 99% people poor, compared to the 1% rich, and have to 'occupy wall street '?

In the 1960s, in the wealthiest country of the world, the USA, for 100 people starting their career at age 25, by the time they reach 65, the following would have occurred : 28 will be dead, 15 will be broke, 47 will be barely getting by, only 10 will be somewhat okay. Very few, less than 1%, will be rich.

In 2016, in the USA, the 100-person story goes like this : 13 will be dead, 10 will be broke, 65 will be just getting by, only 12 will be somewhat okay. Less than 1% will be rich.

The last 50 years have not changed much, except a longer life span. This makes life insurance rates go down and health insurance rates go up. Since people will live longer and life insurance premiums will be paid for a long, long time. In addition, the people will need more medical care, and for a long time, the cost of which is getting more and more expensive day by day.

This has been happening in the richest land in the history of the civilization. US public has had plenty of help from talk show hosts, financial planners, scores of stock brokers, and money managers, and the great brokerage houses, in addition to hundred of financial newsletters. Can we, thus, argue that all those mentioned above work for the big corporations, sell advertisements, magazines, newsletters, and are merely financial entertainers, to keep the public at large poor.

Because of the advise they receive from these financial Gurus, and the public's interest in following shady advice, we are in this financial mess. These financial institutions, really help big banks and the wall street to succeed at the cost of 99% of us, and themselves belong in the 1% affluent. No wonder, someone said, ' The best way to loot a bank is to own one'.

⑦
Charitable Giving

For the last several months enormous amounts of money has flown into charitable causes the world over and it is said that the appetite for 'giving' is huge. This should help alleviate some of the problems of the world, especially in developing countries, and support numerous noble causes at home.

Advisors need to present 'Charitable Giving' to their employer/ groups clients, as the time is very favorable for such a discussion and the tax implications and benefits to the society at large enormous. Below are some facts, I mention to my group clients on charitable giving, and for setting up a private foundation. Sometimes I make a few peanuts out of the giving program, but most of the time the job is completely voluntary, and provides me with satisfaction of enhancing the cause of charity.

Charitable giving maximizes the support to the causes one cares about. Giving is one of life's greatest satisfactions. It allows you to share your financial success with loved ones and establish a legacy to benefit future generations. Before making a gift or donation, one needs to know some facts about charitable giving to maximize the benefits of the gift to the recipient and save undue costs.

Gifts are irrevocable. The donor must release all control and title over the asset for the gifting process to be complete. Gifts can trigger taxes. Gift taxes are levied on donor, not the recipient. Most gifts are tax-exempt. Five gifts that do not trigger gift taxes are: Any gift to a spouse, in any amount, because there is an unlimited marital deduction provision. Spouses should be US residents/citizens. Gifts up to $14,000 (for tax year 2016) a year, per donor/recipient to any number of individuals. This is called annual exclusion. The gift should be available to the recipient for Immediate use/ possessions / enjoyment or spouse's gift that follows the above rule to the same individual(s). The total annual exclusion to a married couple is, thus, $28,000. The IRS considers them to be split gifts- $14,000 from each spouse.

Gifts to charities and/or political organizations. These may have ramifications, however, the wise donor uses caution with such gifts.

Paying medical and/or educational/tution expenses for other person, especially when it is directly to the institution(s). To quaity as a gift, transfer during one's lifetime, of cash, securities, property or any other kind of asset should be permanent and irrevocable. Some gifts may require the donor to pay a gift tax. These could be : Amounts over the annual exclusion of $14,000 or $28,000 to any individual in a single year.

Any gift of any size not available to the recipient for immediate Use/enjoyment/possession, Medical and/or educational/ tution expenses not paid directly to Institution concerned. If one makes a gift that is taxable, the IRS requires you to file a gift tax return, IRC form 709, and keep copies indefinitely. Filling the gift tax return does not mean one has to pay gift tax, which is at about 55% rate currently. Presently we all have a lifetime exemption equivalent to about $5 Million.

Hence large gifts will reduce our lifetime exemption and decrease our liability to estate taxes at the time of our death, by the amount gifted. A future increase in exemption limits, a repeal of estate taxes, imposition of higher/newer state taxes and other provisions in the tax rules after the year 2016 are still undecided, and being discussed by the congress. With proper planning today, one can realize immediate tax benefits,enhance the quality of life for loved ones, and increase the scope of some organizations, by gifting. Even with modest amounts, one can create a foundation or join many of the foundations already established for charitable giving programs. Creative gift giving can lower the overall taxes for the donor, and benefit loved ones and favorite causes. Gifts or transfers of assets to minors (UGMA/UTMA), children, grand children have been popular for a long time. New education and college savings plans have extended the scope of giving even further. In addition to children/grand children, gifts can be designed to take care of the long-term needs of parents/ grand parents on a tax-deductible, tax-favorable basis.

To secure current and future income for yourself and loved ones and enable one to leave a philanthropic legacy, one can setup a tax-deductible annuity program. Many such legitimate and excellent programs are available. A qualified tax attorney, a financial planner, or competent accountant can provide further insight into charitable giving.

The paperwork on these programs usually are simple and easy to execute. For complicated estates, charitable remainder lead trusts and other instruments may be designed to manage funds in tax-efficient ways to provide the maximum benefit to all concerned.

(8)

Charity

Charity, philanthropy and giving is in the air at year end.

We exchange gifts, offer food, toys and clothes to the needy and hungry, in addition to our loved ones.

The amount of charitable giving declined in 2008 and 2009, than at any times in the last 50 years, by 15%. 2010 has seen charitable giving gone up by 11% and is back to normal levels.

Nonprofits, or tax-exempt organizations, classified 501(c), are required to file form 990 to IRS. After missing to file this form for three consecutive years, these organizations, loose their nonprofit status.

275,000 such nonprofits lost their federal tax exemptions in 2010. It may be prudent to confirm with IRS, before sending your donations to an organization, if they are still qualified.

A total of $300 billions or more are given to charity every year, mostly by individuals, almost $212 billion, 70% of total given. Corporations, Foundations and Bequests added another $88 billion. Many educational, cultural, religious, and environmental organizations depend upon charity for their existence.

We all need to provide funds for charity, as giving is the greatest source of pleasure, and supports the causes one cares about. There are significant tax-advantages and tax deductions available to donors.

One can set up foundations and charitable accounts where donations are tax-deductible, and donor can later receive a majority of the funds, thus collected over the years, returned to the donor, at very tax-favorable terms.

(9)

Credit Score

One generally needs a (big) loan to begin, operate and expand a business. Lenders, banks, mortgage brokers (for both residential and commercial purposes) always ask for credit score. Fair Isaac Corporation, introduced in 1989, the FICO score, the most commonly used measurement to evaluate an individual's ability to repay a debt.

It ranges between 300-850, and the 'score' can be obtained, at www.myfico.com. A free credit report, (which does not include a credit score), once a year, from the three major reporting agencies (Equifax, Experion, and TransUnion) is available by calling. 1-877-322-8228, or by visiting www.AnnualCreditReport.com which is sponsored by Credit reporting bureaus.

Credit scoring has been in existence since 1950s, introduced by large retail departmental stores and financial instiutions to support their lending practices. A higher credit score allows one to obtain more favorable payment terms, while the lower score results into less favorable terms. Lower the score, bigger the risk for repayment of debt for the lender.

Higher credit score can help with better options, like lower interest rates, and loan terms eventually saving funds to the borrower. It always, thus, helps to improve/increase ones' credit score. If you have a million dollars in a Bank and have never taken a loan, your credit score will be very low, as the lenders do not have a history of your repayment of a loan, and can not determine your loan-worthiness. On the contrary, if you have only twenty five thousand dollars in bank, have taken (several) loans in the past, and have repaid them on agreed terms, and within stipulated time, your credit score could be very high.

This is why people who have arrived in US, just a short time ago, may not succeed getting a loan without a substantial down payment, due to lack of credit history.

The credit score is determined by several factors, which have different values : payment history (35%), amounts owed (30%), length of credit history (15%), types of credit in use (10%), and new credit (10%). Credit score can be improved, by: 1. making timely payments on an existing financial obligation, and 2. reducing the amount of debt (revolving credit) one already has. Moving credit around, like borrowing from one credit card to pay for another credit card, actually decreases credit score.

Having fewer loan/credit accounts enhances the credit score, while opening more and more accounts reduces the credit score. Disputing and getting incorrect information removed from ones' credit files helps improve the score.

Managing credit, and maintaining high credit score is complicated and difficult to accomplish. However there are several credit counseling services that help in improving ones credit score, getting people out of debt, and help stay on track for future financial transactions.

Federal Credit Reporting Act (visit www.nfcc.org and www.ftc.gov/credit), FCRA promotes the accuracy, fairness and privacy of information. Since Identity Theft has become a menace, one should be prudent in Protecting ones' credit score.

(10)

Creditor-Protection

Business Owners and Professionals can lose wealth as a result of creditors and Judgments from Lawsuits.

With advance planning and proper measures one can protect, some or most of their assets, and make it difficult for creditors to reach them. To become 'Judgment Proof' will require tax and legal advice and fees to the Experts, but should be worth the time, effort and money.

Here are a few suggestions :

Increase errors and omissions and liability coverage(s), including an Umbrella Policy.

Incorporate your Business, and do not conduct as sole Proprietor or General Partner. Create Multiple Business Entities, so that debts and liabilities of businesses do not cross transfer.

Own business employment and fiduciary insurances, to combat claims by employees. Create wealth in Qualified retirement plans, protected under ERISSA, exceptions IRS and Quadro.

Form IRA Rollover plans, protected by State, not ERISSA, Employee Retirement Income Security Act. Title Assets in Spouse's name, but divorce and Quadro, Qualified Domestic Relations Order may affect.

Joint tenancy arrangements with spouse may be exempt from creditors, except when both have same debtor.

Prepare an Asset Protection Trust, APT, as a Grantor, with investments, with an independent trustee.

Wealth should be created as : Primary Residence, Cash Value Life Insurance, and Deferred Annuities.

Asset protection planning should not be fraudulent, and should not be to defraud creditors. Proper tax and legal advice must be obtained. Becoming financially solvent, becoming debt free, and creating Wealth in exempt ways will generate 'Well Planned Estate(s)' and improve Cash Flow for ever.

Defined Benefit

The defined benefit pension plan is the classic solution pre-scribed for older business owners and professionals with tax problems. It allows larger initial plan deposits (and tax deductions), and still accumulates interest on those funds tax free until retirement.

Yet, thanks to a large population of aging baby boomers who need to save big bucks in a short time and repeal of the 1.0 calculation under 415(e), those in the know would tell you that the defined benefit plan is making a comeback. The 412 plan, because of its simple administration and high initial tax deductions, is leading the plans.

412 Who ?

In real language, it's a "fully insured" plan; that is, one that's funded exclusively by insurance or annuity contracts. Insurance has been considered by some a less-than-effective funding vehicle, so what makes this version of the defined benefit plan more attractive?

First, 412 plans play it safe: they involve no investment risk and they guarantee all benefits.

Second, because all values are guaranteed by contract, Section 412 of the irc (Internal Revenue Code) hence the plan's name exempts such plans from the funding (and filing) requirements that complicate uninsured and split-funded defined benefit plans.

Finally and here's the real plus-the fully insured plan's conservative funding and investment assumptions tend to generate larger initial contributions and deductions than regular defined benefit plans.

For example, the first-year contribution (to fund the maximum allowable benefit) for a 60-year-old in a 412 plan can be 17% larger than that provided under a standard defined benefit plan. And the advantage is greater for participants with more years to accumulate deposits. The 50-year old gets a 26% advantage!

Annual deposits start high and decrease each year. A perfect plan for the owner who wishes to "wind down" the business as he or she approaches retirement.

Who Needs A 412 Plan ?

A 412 plan is not for everyone. But the same people who would (tax laws notwithstanding) gain the most from a standard defined benefit plan would also find a 412 plan attractive. Specifically, someone who:

1. is a small-business owner with one to five employees;
2. is over age 50;
3. has a profitable business with a stable earnings history;
4. wants to maximize contributions and deductions while avoiding IRS entanglements.

Complete Services At No Separate Cost

As with all qualified plans, there is the need for competent plan design, carefull installation (to avoid those IRS audits), and annual reviews (to keep the plan provisions and coverages in compliance). Berkshire Life combines these services with knowledgeable people at our local agencies and at no separate cost to the client!

So, despite what you may have heard to the contrary, defined benefit plans are alive and well. It's just a mater of knowing where to look!

Disability

In the beginning of my insurance career, a colleague told me about a client in California who sued an agent for not discussing disability insurance (DI) when the agent sold him a life insurance policy. The client alleged that he would have bought DI if he had been told about it. He became disabled a few years after buying the life insurance policy, and his lack of income made it impossible to pay the life insurance premium. In addition, the life policy had no waiver of premium rider.

Since then I never have left DI out of my discussion with even a single prospect, whether I speak about life, pension, health, or any kind of insurance or investment products.

Based on the literature I collected at Million Dollar Round Table (MDRT) meetings, I developed a one-page disability explanation, which I call the "Rescue Helicopter." I use the flier when I present the need for a disability policy to a prospect and also keep a copy in the folder that I use to deliver the disability policy to my clients. I have mailed or faxed this sheet to prospects many times, and I occasionally receive a call about the "airplane" policy. The helicopter image sometimes sticks in prospects' minds as an airplane.

Rescue Helicopter

You have a great business/profession. You have adequate life insurance, good income, and substantial long-term security through a pension plan... provided that you make it to the retirement date.

As long as you are working, your income will continue. You have a secure future. Your life insurance will take care of your family if you die prematurely. Your pension plan will continue during your retirement. What it you can't keep working up to the date when your pension begins?

It's like climbing a mountain. The peak is reached when you retire. The climb is easy, because you are fit and well. If your health is impaired and you can't work, you will be stuck at the bottom of the hill and three is no way up.

We can arrange for a rescue helicopter to be standing by, just in case. If you can't work for some reason, we will call in the helicopter, pick you up, and place you on top—exactly where you would have been if you had made it all the way by yourself.

Because I know that my prospects have a greater chance of being disabled than of dying, I am satisfied every time I place a disability policy. I feel good about taking care of my prospect's income protection. I explain that health insurance pays for the hospital and physicians and that life insurance pays to care for his or her loved ones, but only DI pays directly to the prospect, helps keep his morale high, and is a kind of self-respect insurance. A retired person also should cosider long-term care and home health care insurance in his DI needs.

The DI may seem to be an easy topic, because everyone needs DI. Professionals and business-owner prospects especially need to protect their incomes. DI, however, can be complicated.

Prospects object on many grounds. My natural market is the Indian market, in which brothers and sisters are expected to take care of family members who are in distress. Brothers who own businesses jointly do not like to purchase DI, business overhead protection, or disability buy-out plans. They argue that their partnership will continue unabated and that each brother will take care of the other in case of disability. They do not believe that there is a need to shift this burden to an insurer and pay for it unnecessarily. But IRS and DOL are against those arrangements.

Some prospects even say that they would go back to India if they became disabled because the cost of living is much cheaper there and that their meager Social Security benefits would be enough to survive on comfortably.

Other than affluent physicians, who easily agree to buy disability plans to protect their income, even such rich multi-millionaire Indian business owners as the president of a computer company or a five-star hotel owner avoid buying disability coverage because they say that they will self-insure. They believe that their partners and family members will keep them on the payroll forever. They also may believe that the DI premium money is wasted, as with health and automobile insurance, and that the disability insurance premiums are too high, especially compared to term life insurance.

Professionals who work for large corporations buy only the employer-paid short- or long-term disability coverage, because it is offered at inexpensive group rates and is issued without any underwriting hassles. They refuse to buy personal, own-occupation coverage that has residual benefits or future enhancements without evidence of insurability.

A common question is why DI premium costs 13 times the price my prospects may get from their medical association, dental association, or engineering association, or through AAA. I ask why a Mercedes, which most of these physicians, business owners, and professionals drive, costs more than a Honda.

My comparison may not cut ice with prospects at first. I point out that automobiles with ABS brakes, sunroofs, leather seats, cruise control, sports packages, and compact disc players cost more than those without the extra features. While it is easy to explain this concept to my prospects. DI policies also come with options and features that will make the policies perform differently when a claim is filed or that it can shape the protection that the policies provide.

Negative press that paints the agent as a dishonest salesperson who tries to sell expensive policies only to make larger commissions is another reason for prospects' disbelief. Some agents look at a competing agent's proposal and drop a few features to make their policy premiums appear to be less expensive without explaining the reduced benefits or use misleading statistics to show that their insurance company is better than the competing insurance company. I believe that the trend is to push variable insurance products in place of whole life insurance and not to address DI and other products for the average prospect.

Some insurance companies offer a premium refund option. This option encourages many of my prospects to buy disability coverage because they are sure that it they will not be disabled, the DI premiums they pay will be returned to them. The kinds of premium refund options include :

- A full 100% of the premiums will be refunded if the policy is in force until age 65. The prospect would lose only the interest on the premium funds.

- There is no refund for the first 5 years, after which time a gradually increasing portion of premium is available for withdrawal, similar to a universal life policy's cash value.

- The disability policy can be purchased with or without a premium refund option. The premium refund option costs more, as it returns a portion of the premium with some enhancement factor every five or 10 years. If the prospect waits for a longer period, the refunds will be larger.

The first two kinds of premium refund options are available as extra features with some insurance companies and are unavailable through other insurance companies.

With the third kind of refund option, which I believe is a true premium refund option, the insured pays an extra premium to receive the funds. The internal rate of return (IRR) on such cases is about a 12% to 15% on the extra premium paid.

There are two schools of thought regarding own-occupation, non-cancelable policies and the premium refund option. Some agents believe that the premium refund option is of no use because prospects could put the same funds that they would use to purchase a premium refund option into a mutual fund and obtain a better return on their investment. Other agents believe that if the prospect does not use or sparingly uses the policy, the guaranteed return of premium is an excellent feature that makes the DI policy similar to a whole life policy with future cash values. I belong to the latter group. Mutual funds are not guaranteed, and I believe that a 12% IRR makes great sense if the prospect does not use the DI policy.

Not all top-rated DI companies offer premium refund options. I find that it is easier to sell DI policies from insurance companies that include this option, especially in my niche market where savings are more prevalent than buying insurance. This is why the combination of buying term life insurance and investing in the stock market is less common in the ethnic markets than in the average United States population. In ethnic markets, prospects are likely to invest in the stock market regularly through mutual funds or individual stocks, but they also buy whole life insurance because it is an excellent way to invest in addition to providing insurance protection.

Only a few insurers that offer non-cancelable, own-occupation policies compared to numerous excellent life insurance companies, it is clear, convincing testimony to show how tough the disability market is. There are few insurance companies that can handle DI coverage well, so there is not much scope for comparison-shopping on policy features and premiums.

I have succeeded in selling DI plans with a premium refund option to affluent prospects. I carry, mail, or fax a copy of a check that I have received as a premium refund from my insurer, both on personal disability and business overhead policies, to prospects to remind them that this valuable feature works and what kind of refund is available to them.

A prospect who insists on buying term insurance and investing the difference and who regularly invests in the stock market is not a good candidate for the premium refund option. A prospect who buys a whole life insurance policy and who does not invest frequently, however, usually is interested in a return of premium option on his DI policy.

The merger of several top disability insurance companies into one, and the trend for insurers to get out of own-occupation contracts has made issuing DI policies more difficult. More stringent underwriting has made the agent's job more complex. Only about six top-rated insurance companies are in the DI market, and some of the aggressive and major players are out of the market or have sold their block of business to companies that have been able to manage the ratio between premium collection and claims payment more realistic.

Many more innovative products are being made available for the DI market. I believe that the sale of DI policies should become easier as prospects understand how difficult it is to get the coverage issued.

The few insurance companies that still offer the premium refund or return of premium option should be well sought after by agents. Companies that do not offer a return of premium, but that are well known and are major players in the DI market, have alternatives to offering refund of premium. An example is to offer a refund of premium feature through a life insurance policy, in which the policy's cash value may be used for return of premium. In such a case, two policies must be offered: a DI policy and a universal, whole life, or even variable insurance policy. Withdrawals from the life insurance policy will be arranged to mimic the return of premium.

If the agent becomes aware of the premium refund feature's appeal to his prospects, he can give his prospects more reasons to buy DI coverage.

(13)

Double Agent

While buying real estate, residential, commercial or land, we often deal with a 'Double Agent'. The agent who does research, finding us a proper property, who shows us the homes and buildings, and spends countless hours with us, for weeks, months, sometimes years, is working for the Enemy, the Seller, may not be obvious to many of us. This is true for all the agents, we locate from a 'For Sale' sign, in the subdivision, sitting and selling new homes, or the ones who pick you up and become your free tour guide of the city. In them you confide so much, reveal all your secrets, explain all your needs, show your bank statements and provide your tax-returns, who chooses a lender and an attorney for you to make the deal go through. They all are 'double agents'. It looks like they work for you, the buyer, but they don't, they work for the seller.

The agent who puts his name and information on a 'for sale' sign on a property, is called the 'Listing Agent', or Seller's Agent. The agent who works with the buyer, is called a 'Selling Agent', or Buyer's Agent. Both agents, listing- and selling- are normally paid by the seller. Listing Agent is paid for marketing the property, and the Selling Agent for procuring a qualified and willing buyer. Buyers normally do not normally pay for the services of any of these agents, selling or listing (buyer's or seller's). Hence none of the agents look after the interests of the buyer. Both the agents consider buyers, as a customer, and treat them fairly and honestly. While the seller is a client for both the agents, as seller pays for their services, hence seller's interests need to be protected by both the agents, otherwise there could be a breach of contract or illegal activity. None of the agents have any loyalty nor contract with the buyer, has to be kept in mind. Have you heard, 'my realtor is so good, he/she got me this home/property at such a great price/terms' from a happy buyer ? This statement is so far away from the truth and kind of illusionary. If this were true, seller can sue both the agents for the breach of contract, for collusion to sell his/her property below cost, and at unfavorable terms. Realtors, themselves, also, unknowingly try to dupe their prospects and buyers, by proclaiming this fact. Buyers feel so happy hearing, 'it is a good buy'. Both agents want the property to sell as fast as possible, procure as much funds, in sale proceeds, as possible, for the benefit of the seller(s), and eventually get paid as soon as possible. However, the buyer's agent has to fairly and honestly deal with the buyer(s), provide information that does not harm the seller, helps finding inspectors, attorneys, mortgage brokers and tax-advisors to the best of his/her ability, but can not guarantee any of their acts and efforts for the buyer. Like the seller's agent, the buyer's agent also has to keep the interests of the seller, above all else, their own and that of buyer.

In most states the agent you have hired to find and sell you a property, represents the seller. In many states the dual agency, one agent/broker representing both buyers and sellers, is prohibited by law. When we walk into a subdivision and buy a home, or call from a sale sign and work with the listing agent, the buyer is allowing a dual agency, means the same agent represents both buyers and sellers. A realtor has numerous other expenses, maintains relationship with numerous loan officers, attorneys, insurance agents, inspectors and engineers, and handymen to create a team of professionals, to complete the arduous transaction, should eventually agree to refund a portion of his/her fees collected from the seller, with the buyer?

It does not make sense. A selling agent who succumbs to such pressures from the buyers, to acquire more buyers and get more business, will eventually fail, and will not last in the business long enough. Even if he does, he will make such a poor living, and will not have the means or resources to rise to the level of an experienced and competent agent. This will eventually hurt the cause of the buyer. Such an agent can be of no help, if there be any defect in the property or there is a flaw in paperwork, detected years later.

Dynasty Trust

Here is the 100 year plan to create wealth, which the super affluent(s), like Rockefellers, DuPonts, Kennedys, Tatas, Birlas, Ambanis and others have successfully implemented.

It may be useful to plan doing so even with smaller amounts and get big results.

The parent is assumed to die in 25 years from now. The child dies in 50 years, the grand child in 75 years and the great grandchild in 100 years.

$1 Million invested at 5% net, without the trust will be $5 Million, after 100 years while with The Family Dynasty Trust will Grow to $131 Million, after 100 years, since no taxes will be taken away.

(15)

Education Funding

Education makes a person better. It helps one earn more money, makes people more useful to the society. But the 'education', especially good quality, at fine Instittutions is expensive, and is getting more and more expensive, day by day. Investing funds, for the use of children, for current and future educational expenses has to be, hence, very prudent.

I will try to narrate my approaches, that I have used for my clients, and my own children and grand children over the last 25 years or so.

I wiill describe them under 3 different headings :
1. Life Insurance,
2. Education IRA
3. College Savings Plan

Insurance : Whenever a child is born to a client, a propspect, a family member, etc I rush to set up a life insurance on the child called juvenile insurance, within 3-4 months of the birth of the child. Many a people do not like the idea of buying insurance on the life of a child, and hate to think of profiting from the prospect of death of a loved child. But I generally succed in setting up a $100,000 juvenile life ins policy on a child, who is less than 1 year old. The premium would be about $5 per month. But I ask the parent to overfund the policy by paying $100 to $200 per month. In 5 years, by paying $10,000 or so, the policy is paid for life. The life insurance due to accumulated cash value may become worth $500,000 or even $1 Million, by the time the child is 22 years old, has finished college, has a job, is planning to marry, and needs to buy life insurance, if premium payments are continued. The policy can

(41)

be surrendered, and the cash value, could be about $25,000 at age 18 of the child, can be used to pay for college tution. The premium payment can be suspended for 4-6 years, untill the child has a job, say around age 24-25, and he/she then can resume premium payment, increases the value of the policy, withdraw funds to buy a car, get down payment for buying a home, eventually turn it into a tax-free retirement plan for age 65 onwards, and create huge financial legacy for heirs, charity and posterity. The premium paid at age 1 of the child remains same until age 121. There is never a medical exam, and any adverse medical conditions that may develop over the life of the child will never matter, as it is a continuous policy from age 1 to age 121, if one can manage it properly.

Savings Account : The Covedell Educations Savings IRA, also known as ESA, Education Savings Account, allows parents and others to put a maximum of $2000 per year per child/student. The funds are not tax deductible but grow tax-deferred and can be taken out tax-free, both principal and earnings. The account eventually belongs to the child, and the ownership is transferred to the child at his/her age 18. This plan is available in all States of the Union. The beneficiary on the account can be changed before the child turns 18, and the funds can be used for the expsnes of the school, including private schools, as well as for the college. Amounts not used for educational purposes are penalised. The accumulation of $2000 a year to even age 18, will not generate enough funds to send a child to Harvard, Yale, or Stanford. Henec more funds need to be invested to fund a college education properly.

College Plan : College Savings Plan(s) are also called 529 Plans (irc, internal revenue section 529) and vary from State to State. One can put $250,000 or more (in several instalments) for each child into the plan to generate enough resources to take the child through 4 or more years of undergraduate and graduate school(s) at the finest of institutions. Some states provide limited tax advantages, if the parents keep the funds in their own state's 529 plan. Parents can, however, ignore this trap and put their funds in the best state's plan and with the best custodians. We are allowed to invest in the 529 of any of the 50 state of the union and use it in any state's school where the child goes to study. The funds are not tax-deductible, with certain exceptions, but grow tax-deferred and come out tax free if used for college education. Not using the funds for college funding will trigger penalty by IRS. The benficiary on the plans can be changed by owners/parents.

Final Thought : Any of the 3 plans outlined above will destruct itself, if funding is not continued for a suffcient number of years. Hence parents need to have adequate life, disability and other insurance policies and enough savings, to cover the payments. Many a times it is better to setup the 529 plan in the name of parents themselves, even if they do not plan or need to get continuing education, and eventually transfer funds for the benefit of children or others as and when the needs arise. This is a smart estate planning tool also.

Eleventh Commandment

Is it a cardinal sin to be paid to help investors choose the right mutual fund? Is it true that no load funds are saintly, or that commissions are sinful ? At time when investors sorely need personalized attention and encouragement, selling load funds is not a sin. Load is not a burden, rather a trust clients place in financial professionals and the responsibility the financial institution takes in performing sound investment decisions.

No-loads are not no-load. They collect fees over a longer period of time, but collect fees they do! Who pays for all those no-load advertisement in the popular financial press? Put your money in a bank savings account and earn 2% interest with no load. who pays for the salary of the bank employees and for other expenses of the bank ? Pay a 3% sales charge to mutual fund manager and receive a dividend of 12%, not guaranteed of course. No-load benefit is for short term, say one to five years. The commission fund charge lower fees and perform much better in long run. So, load funds in a properly exccuted financial plan will prove less expensive.

Obtaining the services of a fee charging professional and a no-load clerk will definitely show different results within a very short span of time. The principle of risk versus reward in achieving a definite financial goal can be managed with prudence by only a professional. A good professional planner who puts clients' interests first survives longer and will earn more fees. The real question is not fees. It's result. The valid comparison is not what a client might have done in a no-load versus commission fund, but rather what the client would have likely done without a financial professional's help.

Arguments in favour of no-loads are largely emotional that their advocates have artfully disguised as factual. Who likes to work for free or even afford to do so? Is it fair to ask someone to work for free? If an investor wants, personalized, quality, financial services he must pay. When you get the check in the restaurant, you could just sign the credit card slip and leave, but you don't. Instead out of courtesy you add 20% or more for the waiter. Why should you complain about the 4.5% commission? In some cities, if you left 4.5% tip, the waiter would chase you down the street.

To judge load properly, the entire fee structure charged over the anticipated life of the investment should be compared with the full value received. Have you ever noticed the sign in any store window reading. "We sell at cost"? How would one make money selling at cost? The answer is, "Buy for less than cost".

the biggest illusion is that one can buy the same service or investment package for a consistently lower price. Continuing advise over the years, pericdic review, newer recommendations and adjustment of portfolio to meet the changing needs and the changing times for achieving financial goal is valuable and will cost. Many investors need encouragement to invest in the first place. Almost all need their hands held during short term reversals in the market. there are no free lunches and when thing sound too good to be true, they usually are not.

Sixty percent of the price of Kellogg's corn flakes goes to distribution and marketing. You might prefer to walk into a store and buy a generic brand labeled "Corn Flakes" to reduce the load. An extermist may even be frustrated that they can't grow Corn on the Balcony of their apartments. For some, there may be no value in distribution and the average person should be left to find or create the best products on his own. Value and quality, not just the price, always count.

17

Employee Bonus, Section 162

Employers and Business Owners provide many benefits to their employees for better production, high morale and for eventual profit to the Business. Almost everyone, called Rank and File, gets basic benefits, like safe and secure workplace, group benefits like medical-, dental-, vision-, life-, and disability-insurance. In addition, a retirement plan goes a long way to keep employees stick longer at their place of employment. This helps the businesses minimize attrition, and avoids the problem(s) of hiring and re-training employees.

But the key employees, managers, middle managers and those group leaders who interact with the rank and file regularly, and keep the business running smoothly, need extra incentives. These incentives can be structured under Section 162 of the IRC, internal revenue code, as Bonus.

Let us imagine, two job situations. In the first the monthly salary paid to the employee/manager is $5000 per month and no benefits. In the second, the monthly salary is $4500 a month, $500 less every month, $6000 less every year, $55,000 vs. $60,000 per year. But the second job comes with benefits. If employee or their family members are sick, they get medical/dental/vision care. If the employee is unable to work due to accident or sickness, he/she is paid, tax-free salary of $3000 per month to age 65, when social security should take over. In case the employee dies prematurely, his/her family is paid a sum of $1 Million tax-free.

If the employee works for a long time and reaches age 55-65, he/she gets a pension of $7000 per month for life, including retiree medical benefits.

Most of these employee benefits, when paid by the employer, are tax-deductible. These benefits and payments should also be non-discriminatory, available to all the employees, without any discrimination, or they loose their tax-deductible status.

But extra incentives, bonuses, for key employees and managers (including owners) can be discriminatory, and provided to only a few. If these are provided to all rank and file, it will create a huge financial burden for the Business/ Corporation, and may not be profitable to the business. Hence some incentives and bonuses have to be designed for only key employees and owners. If these incentives are tax-deducted by the corporation, they must be added to the key-employees' income and become taxable to the employee or manager, since they are discriminatory. If the business or employer provided these incentives to their key-employees and owners, and does not tax-deduct them for the corporation, the benefits become available tax-free to the key-employees, and owners, even if they be discriminatory.

Many a times the employers provide a double bonus, which helps the corporation to deduct the bonus as tax-deductible business expense, and the entire bonus also becomes tax-free to the key-employees and owners.

By the same token, Business Owners can provide enormous bonuses to themselves without including, even key-employees, managers or rank and file, if they structure it properly.

To avoid unnecessary attacks on bonus plans by IRS (Internal Revenue Service) and DOL (Department of Labor), corporations should adopt an official resolution, indicating why the plan is being adopted and to whom plan benefits are being provided.

18

Estate Planning

What is an Estate, and what is Estate Planning? Estate Planning is a part of Financial Planning, which takes care of things and finances after you are gone, and leaves your estate for your heirs. Everything one owns : cash, investments, real estate, properties, businesses, royalties all together make up one's estate. People set up wills and trusts to manage their estate after they leave for 'heaven'. If you die without a will, you die 'intestate' and the State/Government will determine how to dispose of your estate.

A well documented Will (and trust) makes life easier for everyone, as specific instructions are provided in the Will to distribute assets to heirs and/or charity.

However, the State may still conduct a probate, to establish the validity of the will, and allow disposal of properties, afterwards. It is always a good idea to avoid probate.

Estate Planning is not only for super-rich. A person of modest means, with a house valued at $300K, and a life insurance policy of $1 million, and couple of hundred thousand in a pension plan, and a small business valued at $500K, will total to a estate of $2 million or so, and will trigger an estate tax of $800K, at 40% rate. Estate Planning, thus helps in designing plans to minimize or elminate this estate-tax after death, also called, 'death tax', or 'success tax', or 'generation-transfer tax' and is different from income tax. This planning is done with the following objectives in mind :

1.provide fair and biggest possible share of the estate to heirs,

2. generate enough cash to pay for final expenses, taxes, and charity,

3. to save business or property for future generations.

4. to avoid, eliminate and/or hasten the probate process.

5. to avoid any discord amongst surviving family members and business partners.

The planning is done by a team of experts, generally an estate planning attorney, an accountant or CPA, and a financial planner for the benefit of the Client/Prospect and their immediate family members. The basic things one needs for a sound estate planning are :

1. up-dated will,
2. correct beneficiary designations,
3. proper asset allocation,
4. adequate insurance program, like policies inside a trust,
5. powers of attorney for financial and health care issues,
6. a regular gifting program for heirs and charity, and
7. following the changes in tax rules.

A bigger and more complicated estate normally needs several things in addition to the facts mentioned above, which could be :

1. generation-skipping planning,
2. planning for expected inheritance,
3. transferring assets tax-free to children and grand children,
4. survivorship or second-to-die life insurance plans,
5. qualified personal and charitable trusts,
6. family limited partnerships, and,
7. Private foundations.

However, the most common form of estate planning technique is the creation of an ILIT, irrevocable life insurance trust, and placing life insurance policies in the trust, so that the death proceeds, which are generally received income-tax free, can also stay out of one's estate. This is designed based on the wishes of the owner of the estate, and their decision to leave funds for : Family, Charity and Government, after their demise.

The grantor creates an irrevocable life insurance trust, trustee(s) purchase life insurance policies insuring grantor's (and/or spouse's) life, and become(s) the owner and beneficiary of the policy. At grantor's death, trustee(s) receive insurance death benefit, and the Executor of the trust takes care of any probate, follows the spirit of the Will, and distributes funds amongst heirs, charity and the government in the most efficient way(s) possible.

Feminine Side

Indians are celebrating Navaratri, on a big scale the world over. Durga, the Goddess of Shakti, Power is being worshipped, with big fan fare. The rituals associated with Durga are everywhere, including UNO, Madison Square Garden, and White House. Very soon we will be involved with Lakshmi, Goddess of Wealth, and then with Sarasvati, Goddess of Knowledge. The Sanatan Dharma also mentions, 'Yatra Naryastu Pujyante, Ramante Tatra Devata'. Plenty of empowerment for Women. Where women are respected, the Gods live there.

Hence we come to the fact that Women are becoming very significant in Financial matters and are much underserved. It is time we all, especially Male Financial Planners, develop our feminine side of the talent.

Women still make less money than their male counterparts, during their career. Women are the primary caregivers, both at the beginning and at the end of the life, from maternity, to child birth, to serving the elderly, until death. Women live longer, hence there is need of funds for them for a longer period of time.

Women have more health-care costs, and need them for far longer than men do. Many widows are left penniless, since men mostly take straight life pensions, rather than joint life pensions, and may not have adequate life insurance for the surviving spouse.

But financial planners and sales people from any kind of business, need to know, that selling and servicing women prospects and clients needs, special skills.

Women want a relationship, before they buy any service. Women want details of any transaction, before taking any action. Women are savers, and do not like to take unnecessary risk with their finances. They tend to think of providing for the whole family, not for just themselves. Women, deserve and demand, respect.

Most widows change their financial planners, after the husband has passed away, and locate another agent who treats them fairly and better.

Women now control 75% of family finances, 26% earn more than their husbands. Hence it is time to develop more of feminine side of our personality, to succeed, and be useful in sales and service, and attract more female clients.

Financial Balance

Drunk driving is easy to understand, punishable by law, and very stressful, especially when caught. What about Drunk Investing? A large population indulges in it with great pride, obtaining disastrous results, and eventually saying that 99% of the population has to 'Occupy Wall Street' to save us from the financial sharks. Isn't stock market a Casino, to get rich quick, very volatile and unpredictable. Why 90% of wealth is controlled by 10% of the population? Are those 10% rich people crooks and profit on the other 90%? No. The wealthy are smarter and do not indulge in things we 90% do, and repent and become miserable.

The sucessful do not go to Stock Market, and come out into Real Estate and then go into Gold and keep on chasing financial sucess which always eludes them. Laksmi is 'chanchala', always moving, but stays with Rockefellers, Kennedys, Tatas, Birlas, Mittals, Gates, Buffet, Ambanis and their likes, almost for ever.

This example will help explain how we fare in the market. We put $1000 in market by year end we have only $500 left. What was the return,-(minus) 50%. Next year market went up 100%, and our investment is back to $1000. What kind of average return the market had in last 2 years? Minus 50% and Plus 100%, average to plus 75%. How much money the investor made in 2 years, Zero%. Invested $1000, and had $1000 at the end of 2 years. Do not ever fool yourself with the average mathematical return of markets for a 2,5,10,15,20 year or more period(s). Averages are good for charts, but creates poverty, not wealth, and is insane to base your financial plans upon.

It may be prudent to learn the secrets of the affluent and be in financial balance for ever, and never get affeeted by the ripples of the times and markets. It is imperative to learn Financial Organization and move into the top 10%, consequences to the contracry are painful.

(21)

Financial Dis-Organization

Most people, including smart business owners, are financially disorganized. Most try to keep their financial affairs in order, and also strive to keep good records. But most are swimming in a soup of advisors. They ask their friends, and family for financial advise. They contact myriad of professionals for help. They shop continuously for cheaper stuff and inexpensive services. All this presents barriers to success.

While making financial decision people focus on one area. When they look to put money away for children's education, they look for a good college savings vehicle. When they buy a home, they look for a low rate mortgage, with small monthly payments, refinance it in near future, and try to pay it off as soon as possible. When they buy things, they look at their monthly cash flow, and determine if they can afford it.

But every financial decision is interdependent. The past financial decisions one has already made, and those that they will make in future, affects the present financial decision, and complicates the chance of real success.

You might have seen a commercial from a company, someone walking with his number, saying we all have to know a number and should try to achieve it, especially for retirement. This is the biggest fallacy of financial advise. It comes from the book, titled, 'what is your number', and after 150 pages or so concludes that there is 'no way of reaching a definite number for any one' as our lives are very complicated, and full of changes, that occur continuously.

Several domains like protection, assets, liabilities, and cash flow need to be considered together with cost of living, economic forces, goods and services, product wear and tear, life style upgrades, life events etc to achieve a financial balance and avoid financial stress.

We all need to find the person or the system that will charge some fee and provide us happiness, peace of mind, create wealth, and get us out of financial-disorganization.

Financial Fear

Behavioral Finance tells us that we fear high-profile, low probability incidents more, but ignore more immediate risks.

Here are some of the common fears and their probability of occurrence :

Air Travel Accident, 1 in 567,480.
Lightning Strike, 1 in 9,903,437.
Snake Bite, 1 in 50 Million.
Mountain Lion Attack, 1 in 32 Million.
Asteroid, 1 in 250,000.
Spider Bite, 1 in 51 Million.
Shark Attack, 1 in 315 Million.
Dog Attack, 1 in 9,593,955.
Swine Flu, 1 in 383,758.

But the occurrence of financial disasters, has much higher odds, which we fear less and take little notice of : 43% of Americans are 90 days away from poverty, if they loose their job.

Most Americans have less than $25,000 in retirement savings.

Social Security will be exhausted by 2033.

One in six Older Americans, lives below the poverty line.

American Workers are projected to be $6.6 Trillion short of their needs. You spend 12-18% more when you use a credit card, instead of cash.

48% of Americans do not contribute to their workplace retirement plan.

US National debt rises an average of $3.8 Billion per day.

68% of Americans live paycheck to paycheck.

8 in 10 workers plan to continue working in retirement, for lack of funds.

Far scarier than natural disasters, is the real burden of financial risks, we face. We, thus Do not plan to fail, but fail to plan, said someone, for dying too early, living too long, becoming sick and disabled, and running out of money.

Financial IQ

There are complex financial challenges, Entrepreneurs or Business Owners, face them all the time. Lack of financial education and not being able to get financial help, from experts, is kind of sad. We hear, talk-show-hosts pitching, the virtue of saving and not getting ripped off. We are told to shop and compare rates and fees from several vendors before buying any stuff or any service. We also come across numerous advertisements, promising us to save money on insurance premiums, or sell you stuff cheap, from automobiles to homes to clothes and everything else. Yes, there is virtue is saving, and paying less, but most of the time these statements are mere illusion, and far from truth. How can you pay less and less for a service or stuff, that is good, expensive and price-worthy ? It does not exist. A corporation selling better stuff or service at cheap rates will be out of business. Price and value are always relative. Value never comes cheap.

We have been told again and again : Work Hard, Live Below your Means, Save Money, Get out of Debt, Invest for Long Term, and Diversify. Hope you have also heard : Poor Save, Rich Invest. Have you noticed the shrinking middle class, the change of demographics. Rich are becoming richer, while poor are becoming poorer. We used to have 5% rich, 70% middle class, and 25% poor. Now we have 20% rich, 25% middle class and 50% poor. Sure, the virtue of paying less and saving, is a recipe for staying in middle class or slipping into poverty. Business owners and Entrepreneurs, look at their Income and Expenses, analyze their Assets and Liabilities and decide on how to Create Wealth, for themselves, for the society and for future generations.

There are three kinds of people :
1. Do not Invest, are too scared to loose.
2. Invest not to Loose, stay in safe/secure products, for not loosing their shirt.
3. Entrepreneurs, who Invest to Win and Create Wealth.

One has to decide where he/she wants to be in near or distant future.

People in class 1. above stay poor. Those in 2. above, will continue to be in middle class. But a business owner, self-employed, entrepreneur has to take risk, to make it big. Those in 3. above have already taken the risk of leaving a secure, easy job, relinquished having a boss or employer. They need to manage the (financial) risk properly, to achieve their aim and goals in life.

Financial Planning

Financial Planning (FP) is both an Art as well as a Science. Several things are discussed and executed, in this area, based on emotions, feelings and beliefs. While others are decided based on hard facts of taxation, law, and financial expediency. Financial Planners (FPs) practice very specific and individual styles of financial planning, which is as unique as the planners themselves. A Stock-Broker approaches the matter as money management and invests the funds (with obvious risks) for higher gains. An Insurance-Agent is generally interested in setting up insurance plans to avoied future economic losses, and to avoid financial risks. But comprehensive financial planning (FP) goes much further beyond these narrow scopes of 'money management and insurance'. In my optinion, the financial planning should be done with the following two aspects in mind Risk Management, and Investments.

Risk Management, obviously financial, consists of placing mostly insurance policies in force, where an individual or a corporation (business) transfers the risk of financial loss to an insurer (Insurance Company), through payment of relatively smaller premiums, in comparison to the potential bigger, catastrophic economic disadvangates.

The following types of insurances should be planned to avoid losses : Disability-, Accident/Sickness-, Long term care-, Life-, Medical, Dental, Vision-, and property/casualty insurance. Disability Insurance is also called income protection or dignity insurance. Due to sudden accident and illness, one can loose a job or reduce his/her ability to conduct a business, resulting into financial loss, hence an insurance policy should be in place to compensate at the time of such need. It normally covers the active, working life (from age 18 through age 65 or beyond). But a Long Term Care policy covers normally in older times (age 66 through death) agains incapacitation or inability to conduct one's living affairs like eating, transferring from/to bed, toileting and bathing, eventually paying for the expenses or nursing home or home healthcare services.

Medical insurance, including those for accidents, dental and vision-care, covers against sickness and for maintenance of good health for a productive life. Life Insurance generally covers against premature death, in the form of temporary plans (called term policies). This can be coupled with an element of investment, in the form of universal-, whole-, or endowment-policies to manage retirement expenses, and or long term care needs, including in stock market indices. Property and casualty insurances are used to protect automobiles (boats, planes etc), homes, buildings and other structures. They also include coverage for liability, professional malpractice and numerous other things.

For example, the 'wrist' of tennis star, Ivan Lendl, and 'throat' of famous Indian singer, Lata Mangeshkar, were insured for a specific sum, by Lloyds of London, against failing to perform. Investments, require the generation of funds for immediate and/or future use by prudent money management, through small periodic and/or lump sum contributions. this could be done for a comfortable retirement, education planning for children/grandchildren, for charity through foundations for specific causes, general savings for future use, and for immediate and future expenses of any kind, including transferring wealth to the heirs and future generations. This brings into picture the borrowing for home purchase (residential mortgage) or commercial building(s), equipments, for hiring employees and facilities to live properly and conduct a business. It also results into repaying the loans in timely manner and at profitable rates. This will require the services of a stock-broker to invest funds in markets through the purchase of stocks, bonds, mutual funds, REITs, ETFs, and the likes of these, domestically and internationally. A mortgage broker (may be a lender or a bank), should be consulted to make smart decisions about loans and their repayments. An accountant (CPA) should be consulted for tax matters, resulting into favorable tax planning, both for individual and corporate situations. An attorney is needed to set up wills, trusts and other power of attorney documents, for proper conduct of one's affairs, financial or otherwise, in less painful ways, when one is alive and active and when one is gone and has to relinquish the control of things.

A competent Financial Planner, should be aware of the scope and workings of a stock-broker, insurance-agent, realtor, mortgage-broker attorney and accountant, and should have access to all these separate 'hats', and be able to generate a team of professionals to conduct the practice of 'financial planning' effectively.

25

Financial Pyramid

Financial Planning, the path of financial confidence and financial success depends on several simple concepts and their implementation, on a long term basis, fueled by the time value of money.

Any and all available funds need to be divided, in fair proportions, into 3 categories :

Protection, preparation for the unexpected,
Sufficiency, preparation for the expected, and,
Surplus, preparation for more than expected.

Protection, relates to Insurance Contracts, that transfer large financial risks, through the payments of small premiums for home, auto, liability, health, disability, life-insurance and legal documents. Mostly, they are guaranteed promises, and available to be realized at short notices.

Sufficiency, comes from promise based assets, assets based on agreements, like : Bank CDs, Bonds held to maturity, whole life insurance, and annuities. These take some time, generally a decade or so to provide full potential of the promises.

Surplus, depends on market based assets, asset values based on opinion, like stocks, real estate, mutual funds, business ownership, commodities and derivatives.

These are volatile, have no guarantees and can change values quickly, and are influenced by numerous factors, including human emotions.

A proper mix of these 3 different segments in any portfolio is necessary for financial success.

Imagine a pyramid with a wide base of Protection, topped with narrower Sufficiency, and a tapering top of Surplus.

Miracles can be performed, with proper tools and techniques, provided we allow sufficient time for the fruition of goals.

Didn't Archimedes said, ' Give me a long enough lever and a place to stand, and I will move the earth' ?

26

Golden Handcuff

In the beginning of the year, when we receive W2, 1099 (of different kinds), take inventory of income and expenses, and start preparing tax returns. To save on taxes, one has to calculate deductions, business expenses, property taxes, and other matters, bring income to lower brackets, and help avoid paying big in taxes, state and federal. Business owners have to file several returns. 1120 for corporate return before March 15th, and 1040 for personal taxes by April 15th. Both have their state versions too, like forms 500 and 600. Itemized deductions provide more help than standard deduction, in most of the cases.

IRS, Internal Revenue Service and DOL, Department of Labor, allow several kinds of retirement plans to be executed by March 15th and April 15th for the previous year.

One can put $5500 in a Traditional or Roth IRA, older people can contribute $6500. Then there are Simple IRA, and SEP-IRA, where one can shelter up to $52,000 from taxes. Defined-benefits and Defined-contribution plans may allow a business owner to put up to $210K into a pension plan, based on the age and income of the business owner. There is no better way to save on taxes than setting up and contributing into a retirement plan. Business owners and individuals have 3-4 months to compute their income and expenses, and decide on how much to contribute into the retirement plan.

One of the most common retirement plan that business owners setup to help their employees to save money for retirement, and save on taxes is 401(K) plan. Normally the employer matches a portion of the contribution made by the employee and also helps administer the plan. A more liberal plan, and higher matching will keep employees happy, stick longer with their employers, hence it is called golden handcuff.

Small business owners can install even a single person 401(K) plan. A 401(K) plan helps attract and keep talented employees. Employees can decided how much to contribute on pre-tax basis. Contributions made by employees and amounts matched by the employer, both are tax-deductible. Money placed in 401(K) plans can be invested in stock market, in savings accounts or several other vehicles. Even the earnings are not taxed, they are tax-deferred. When an employee leaves the company, they can take their plan to the new employer, or move into their own personal plan.

Employers normally choose one of the 3 plans : Traditional 401(K) Plan, Safe Harbor 401(K) Plan, or Simple 401(K) Plan. Depending upon the number of employees in a company, the number of participants/employees in the plan, and the amount of matching provided by the employer, the kind of plan, most suitable for a particular employer, can be determined.

A trustee has to be located to keep the plan assets safe, a written documents has to be generated to lay the basic rules for the employees, and periodic reporting to participants on their investments is required. Mostly $18,000 to $52,000 per employee per year can be placed inside a 401(K) plan, provided the criteria on participation, matching, non-discrimination, vesting etc comply with the guidelines set by DOL, Dept of Labor. Fiduciary responsibility include the annual reporting to DOL by employers on plan assets, discrimination and vesting schedules. Since the funds have to stay in safe keeping, and will be needed after a considerable length of time, when the employee is ready to retire, strict guidelines are adhered to, and fiduciary, fidelity or erissa bonds need to be in place.

Moving the 401(K) assets away from employer's trustee, to your own personal account, and to withdraw funds from the 401(K) plan at the time of retirement to avoid excessive taxes and make the funds last for a long period in retirement, has several ramifications, and needs expert help.

These plans were started during President Regan's tenure, and have proved to be very popular and useful. No business owner should miss the opportunity of providing a 401(K) plan for the benefit of their employees and the enormous advantages it creates for the business and the employers.

Group Benefits

We have heard the KISS principle many times: Keep it simple, stupid. Speak less. Do not confuse the client. But things in employee benefits are not that simple.

Group benefits are competitive and complicated. Employers shop with several brokers. There is plenty of competition between carriers and brokers to generate enough business. Employers change agents of record for better services and fees. Insurers sell cases directly through the Web, at lower costs and with help from in-house agents.

There are a host of group benefits other than medical, dental and vision plans. We spend numerous hours collecting data and designing and implementing plans. The prices of the plans have to be low, the benefits rich, the renewals predictable, the carrier well known, and the claims quickly paid without any scrutiny. Employers, employees and underwriters have to be satisfied. This demands a lot from the broker.

My recommendation is to present the group benefits, application process, premium calulation, employee enrollment, underwriting and placement of the case as a long, complicated, labor-intensive process. An upfront fee to the agency is in order.

It is not advisable to present yourself as a specialist, such as a brain surgeon, but as a primary care physician who can handle all ailments, and then find specialists to conduct more specific tasks.

It also is not advisable to bring other specialists to the meetings with you. By nature, they will act as adversaries. Sell whatever you can and work on other aspects on your own first. Bring in others, as businss partners, for whatever you cannot do. Referring business to other specialists usually results in loosing the broker-client relationship, as no agent speaks favorably about others. This is what the culture of competition has taught us.

Group benefits should be presented as financial planning for the corporation, with two distinct aspects: risk management and investments.

Risk management

Risk management is simply insurance, and that insurance includes not just property and casualty and business insurance but also medical, dental and vision coverage, short- and long-term disability, long-term care insurance, Medicare supplement and retiree plans.

Then comes life insurance: small amounts on rank and file, group term and supplemental voluntary life for owners and key employees, issued without any medical examination and little underwriting. Dependent insurance must be presented along with employee term life, while non-qualified deferred compensation in the form of split-dollar and corporate owned life insurance needs to be mentioned at the outset.

Presenting these does not take more than 15 or 20 minutes and generates a more sensible census, with names, dates of birth, Social Security numbers, dates of hire and annual compensation. Many times, we succeed in getting two censuses, one prepared for a broker who markets just medical, dental, vision and basic life insurance and one that we, as generalists, have requested. By concentrating on financial planning, we can also ask clients for such things as corporate and personal tax returns in order to generate a more meaningful benefits package proposal. If they feel our information gathering is too exhaustive, we compromise by asking for a less comprehensive census. However, we do not anticipate much business from the group.

This helps in getting a fair share of insurance and investment business from small employers. There is not much need for argument and pushing for data. Those who do not share the information are not ideal prospects anyway, as the fees generated from those employers will not be reasonable enough to justify one's time and efforts.

Investments

Investments should be presented as wealth management for the business I call it "the art and science of financial planning."

Discussions must include retirement plans, not only 401(K)s and 403(b)s but also IRA, Roth, SEP, Simple, profit-sharing, 412, and 419 plans. In some cases, huge amounts of permanent life insurance are needed, although employers and their CPAs normally believe this to be an unsound investment. But life insurance, with its tax-deductible premiums, tax-deferred, growth and tax-free benefits, cannot be matched by any other investment vehicle. Most small business owners will have a hard time investing their funds in a discriminatory way other than in a 419 plan. This is why a high income-generating business also should consider establishing a safe harbor 401(K) plan.

I also speak to employees about their wills, trusts, estate planning and education funding requirements for their children or grandchildren. It is good to visit their CPAs and attorneys when there are chances to place life, disability and longterm care insurance on a agroup or personal basis.

Long-term care and disability insurance are like rescue helicopters. If they cannot work long enough to reach retirement, these policies can place them where they need to be. I have developed some material about estate taxes, LTC and disability, 412 and 419 plans, which I leave for employers who normally whould be interested only in medical and dental benefits.

Most believe you should "buy term and invest the difference." But life premiums on a tax-deductible basis, growth in tax-deferred ways and withdrawal in tax-free mode make high-premium whole and universal policies excellent choices for small employers.

Disability benefits that stop at retirement can continue in the form of long-term care benefits for life, even if a client decides to move temporarily or permanently to a foreign country.

Long-term care coverage can be coupled with life insurance as a rider, and can be purchased as a single-premium policy or for a limited pay plan with premium refund attached to them. Tax-deductible charitable gift annuities can reduce the burden of capital gains for business owners when they dispose of a property and may not recycle funds through their coroprations.

28

Health Care Exchanges

Obama-care is slowly seeping into the body politic of US. If you be liberal, fan of Michael Moore and his movie/documentary, SICKO, and are unhappy that Obama-care does not do enough, and does not provide enough medical care to all, take heart. More is being done for uninsured and those who can not afford medical care and medical insurance. If you are conservative, and do not like the government to pay for medical care and insurance for the poor and uninsured, you are up for surprises, since Supreme Court has backed Obama-care up. And President is bent upon implementing, much of what he has been proposing. Things have gradually changed in the arena of healthcare delivery in US, in 2013, 2014, and beyond.

One of the big things is the establishment of Health care Exchanges by the federal as well as the state governments. It will revolutionize the healthcare benefits for employees, their employers, and those who are not-employed or self-employed, as well as those who do not want to have healthcare insurance.

These exchanges are internet-based sites for purchasing medical insurance coverage. The navigation, selection of plans, and paying for it, will still be complex, hence the insurance agents are still going to be needed to help the public.

There will be two kinds of exchanges, the public exchanges, under PPACA, patient protection and affordable care act, run by governments, and the private exchanges created by private insurance providers.

By 2014, all US states have created two types of exchanges, one for individuals, the other for small employers, called SHOP, small business health options program, with less than 101 employees, participants.

Federal Government will and should support the states in creating the exchanges, which by 2017 can create the exchanges for large employers too. In addition there will be CHIP, children's health insurance program..

Brokers are still needed to help buying public to pick up a proper plan, design the deductible and benefits at affordable rates. Federal Government will regulate and certify the exchanges created by states. Private Exchanges are already in operation, while Government Exchanges, began on October 1, 2013.

29

HIPPA and COBRA

HIPPA is, Health Insurance Portability and Accountability Act of 1996, which became effective on June 1, 1997. It is intended to provide protection from pre-existing condition limitations for employees and their dependents when moving from one job to another job. HIPPA brings with it a complicated chore for Employers and Plan Administrators. It requires that health plans and employers provide with proof or certification of the most recent period of 'creditable coverage' when employees terminate medical insurance and/or move to another job. Penalty for non-compliance are $100 per day, for each individual in a family.

Employers with 20 or more full or part-time employees, who mantain a group health insurance plan, must Comply with COBRA (Consolidated Omnibus Budget Reconciliator Act.) HIPPA is applicable with two or more full-time employees. Employer or Plan Administrator must notify all employees and their spouses of all their rights under COBRA when they first become covered under the group health plan. There are several qualifying events that need to be addressed also. Within 14 days of a qualifying event, employees and spouses must be notified of their continuation rights, benefits and premium rates, and the period of eligibility.

Non compllance with COBRA results into $200 per day, per employee, penalty by DOL, Department of Labor. In addition ERISA (Employee Reetirement Income Security Act) penalty of $100 per day per employee may also be added to it.

Subsequent Congresses have been passing numerous amendments to HIPPA, COBRA and ERISSA Rules at frequent intervals. The current Obama Administration has made sweeping changes in COBRA. It is suggested that Employers and Plan Administrator outsource the compliance, since the rules are complicated, and rigorous ongoing administration is required.

Hot Seat

How do the wealthiest Americans obtain financial advice? How these affluent people manage their money ? They get into a 'hot seat' once every month. They listen to each other on how to save, spend and think about money. This is a club in New York, where these affluent people meet for lunch, spend a few hours together, once in a month, and speak to each other. Most are worth $10 Million plus, and pay a fee of $30,000 a year to meet their peers, just once a month. None inherited their wealth, all of them made their money. One thing they do not do. They do not listen to the advise of financial gurus, do not tune to radio talk show hosts, and do not get their financial advise from TV personalities. They do not believe, in buying cheap financial products. They do not look for, saving a few bucks on insurance premiums and investment fees. They buy the most expensive financial products, available in the market, which perform in superior ways, that creates immense wealth for the members of the group.

Why in the most affluent country of the world, the USA, 90 percent of people after age 65 become poor. They are afraid to retire, fear about medical expenses, worry about outliving their savings, look for another job after retiring, and supplement their income with a second job or a hobby, while young and active and working fulltime, to make ends meet?

Most of them have been sleeping, as they are trying to pursue, the American Dream(s). One can not dream when awake.

Most people try to save, and try hard not to get ripped off. They shop for cheap insurance premiums, and they buy inexpensive stuff, after comparative shopping.

While the smart and successful people, do just the opposite. They locate 'the hot seat', and pay $2500 to sit in it, once a month. They just ignore everything that is available as financial advice in Magazines, Radio, TV and similar sources.

Hubris and Myths

Hubris, means excessive pride or self-confidence, that results into arrogance. We, as financial advisers face this time and again, almost several times a day. Whenever we call upon to acquire a prospect or a client, we are told, 'My financial plans are well set, I do not need any help.' 'I do it myself, with help from a radio or TV talk show host, or consult the financial press'. A physician will not prescribe a medication to cure an ailment, or advise on keeping someone fit, without a physical examination, or without frequent consultation. Financial health, similarly, needs constant help from, and demands payment of adequate fees to an experienced, licensed and well-trained professional. This hubris, and the trust in financial-entertainers, and the following of generic advice, has created a vast majority of financially illiterate people, and the current meltdown. The arrogance leads to downfall, in every area of life, including financial well being.

The affluent and financially successful people do not fall prey to this hubris, and self-help. They do not even believe, in the common Financial Myths, enumerated below :

1. Compounding interest creates a financial miracle.
2. I will be in a lower income tax bracket at retirement.
3. My money only needs to keep pace with inflation.
4. My 401(K) plan creates a tax savings, which can be spent or invested later.
5. I won't need life-, disability- and long term care insurance(s) when I retire.
6. A 15 year mortgage costs less than a 30 year mortgage.
7. Disinvesting, Distribution is same as investing.

8. Return on my assets is more important than regular savings.
9. My cash flow will suffer, by increasing protection.

Add to this, my employer takes care of all my financial needs. I do not need to plan for anything else. Even if you keep a job from age 18 through 65, and retire, 85% of us, who survive, become very poor. And loosing your job, even for a short period, and no plan for financial success, will end in disaster.

Identity Score

An Identity Score, or ID Score, is not the same as a Credit Score, with which most of us are familiar. An ID score is used to confirm a consumers identity and to measure the fraud risk of new customers opening accounts. Car dealers, banks, utility companies, wireless and cable service providers, and many others commonly refer to ID scores. Government regulations will soon require that most businesses use ID scores to identify customers, using it as a means to help combat fraud.

Like the credit score, the ID score attempts to define how disciplined a person is at paying their bills and will also predict the fraud risk of new customer accounts. ID scores are built by collecting information from public and private records, including credit records. Social security number, date of birth, address, phone number, and number of credit applications are combined to calculate and generate patterns and scores for the identity scores.

Changing names due to marriage and/or divorce and living in an apartment complex where several people have similar addresses are two triggers that raise the identity score. A high identity score, in contrast to a high credit score, is considered negative. This results in having to respond to many inconvenient questions when applying for a loan or credit, or while completing business transactions. These challenging questions, such as the color of your first car, and the house number where you lived several years ago, can tax the memory of legitimate consumers. A high identity score can cause the delay or cancellation of a financial transaction.

Major banks and wireless companies are now making identity scores available for consumers to view at MyIDScore.com. This helps consumers assess their personal risk, and is especially helpful in detecting identity theft. The dangers and problems caused by identity theft are often talked about in the media, and are very common, which makes knowing and understanding one's identity score so important.

ILIT

Persons who, over their lifetimes, successfully accumulate an estate made up of cash, CD's, stocks, bonds, real estate (both developed and undeveloped), or a substantial interest in closely held business, face one major problem someday, Estate Shrinkage.

Starting at 37% and going up quickly to 55% and even higher in some circumstances the Federal Estate Tax can destroy a lifetime's efforts, especially if the estate is composed largely of illiquid assets such as real estate.

Having worked with individuals owning estates worth $2 million to estates worth over $100 million, I have found that almost every estate owner falls somewhere within these two extreme positions concerning estate shrinkage.

First Extreme

"I started out with nothing and earned every pefiny I'm worth today. I dont care if my kids end up paying 50% or more to the government in taxes after we're gone. That's a lot more than I had when I started. If they cant' get by on that much, that's their problem, not mine."

Second Extreme

"I've spent a lifetime accumulating an estate and I don't want to pay the government ONE DIME more than I have to. I want to take advantage of every legitimate way there is to avoid estate taxes. My goal is to maximize the property we leave to our children (or charity, grandchildren, etc.) at our deaths."

(83)

Then, of course, there are all shades in between but I've found almost everyone would fall somewhere within these two extreme positions.

The Unlimited Marital deduction which came into being in 1981 essentially eliminated the large Federal Estate Tax problem at the death of the first spouse (regardiess of the size of the estate), but it compounded the problem at the second death.

Asset	Market Value
Home	$325,000
Vacation Property	$150,000
Cash (Savings, Money Market, CD's)	$100,000
Stocks, Bonds	$100,000
Miscellaneous Properties (Cars, Furniture, etc)	$125,000
Pension Assets	$800,000
Value of closely held business interest (80% ownership)	$1,400,000
Total	**$3,000,000**

Estates of this size and larger are more and more common these days.

Assuming the disposition of this property is such that it would be left to Mrs. Sinha at Mr. Sinha's death and the residue to their three children at Mrs. Sinha's death. There would be some taxes, debts, funeral expenses and possibly medical expenses at the first death, but chances are the estate would probably continue to grow modestly and by the second death, could have easily grown to $4 million.

Then at Mrs. Sinha's death, the Federal Estate Taxes could easily approach $2 million (and that's assuming Congress doesn't increase estate taxes rates in near future, which many experts predict is almost a virtual certainty, that it will).

The choices for how to pay these taxes are simple :

1. Dispose of liquid assets (cash, marketable securities: assuming they are marketable at the time of death).

2. Sell other assets (and hope too much isn't tied up in non-liquid real estate, longer term bonds, etc.)

3. Borrow, never try to borrow money from a bank to pay estate taxes, you will be denied.

So, even though the estate might by worth $4 million on paper, having to come up with the money to pay these taxes in nine months when the estate taxes are due, could cause a much greater hardship and much more shrinkage than that caused by the taxes alone.

These are some of the reasons why the "irrevocable life insurance trust" in conjunction with a Joint and Last Survivor Life Insurance Policy has become such a popular estate planning technique.

By designing a life insurance policy that pays off just at the time the cash for the estate taxes is needed (i.e. at the second death), it creates the most cost-effective way of solving the problem.

The technique works for three basic reasons:

1. An irrevocable trust is created which applies for and owns a policy on the two joint lives. By having a properly drawn trust own the policy, the insurance proceeds do not get added to the already existing estate. In other words, a $2 million joint and Last Survivor policy owned by the trust doesn't compound the problem by pushing the size of the estate (i.e. taxes thereon) from $4 to $6 million. The estate stays at $4 million and the additional $2 million of insurance proceeds are available for the beneficiaries (i.e. the children) to use. They

can loan money to the estate to pay estate taxes or they can use the money to purchase assets thereby creating liquidity within the estate.

2. A Joint and Last Survivor policy is considerably less expensive than a single policy on either of the insured individually.

This is true largely due to the significantly lower actuarial probability of the two deaths.

To explain this, it is helpful to take a quick review of the law of probabilities. The chances of rolling a 1 on a single dice is one out of six. When you introduce a second dice, the probability chances change drastically.

The chances of rolling a pair of dice and getting a one on each dice are NOT 2 out of 12, but instead are the product of the individual probabilities multiplied by each other (1/6 X 1/6 = 1/36).

Since each Individual's death represents an independent fractional probability, the product of the two mortality probabilities is much lower than each one's separate mortality chances.

This principle is the primary reason for the cost differential in Last Survivor coverage versus individual coverage on one life. This also explains the cost of a Joint and Last Survivor policy sometimes being lower than the premium on a single policy on the life of a healthy insured even when the second life is totally uninsurable.

3. The premiums for the insurance are made by the irrevocable trust that owns the Last Survivor policy. The husband and wife gift money to the trust each year and because of something known as "Crummey Powers" (named after the court case of the same name), these gifts qualify for the $14,000 annual per person Gift Tax Exclusion ($28,000 for husband and wife). In an example with three children, a hus-

band and wife, both could gift up to about $28,000 each year to the trust.

Not only is the money gifted each year reduces the size of the estate, the entire insurance proceeds which might be several million dollars, should be totally excluded from estate taxation as well.

So, if you're interested in passing the maximum possible percentage of the estate you've managed to accumulate over your lifetime to your family, rather than to the government, you should certainly examine the possibility of an ILIT, irrevocable life insurance trust, funded with a Joint and Last Survivor policy. It's not right for everyone, but it certainly does make a lot of sense in many situations.

34

Inflation

We always hear, work hard, make money. Working hard and making money are kind of synonymous. Larger hours at work makes one earn more. Even those with brilliant ideas, that make one rich, also have to work very hard to achieve their goals. After one has accumulated smaller or bigger amounts of money, we all want our money to work harder, and bring us higher returns, in the form of dividends, interest and profits. This is why CDs are preferable than savings accounts, stocks over bonds, and annuities over insurance. Similarly renting compared to owning.

S&P 500 Index is considered to be the best index of how market is performing, and people getting return on their investment. In 2015 S&P 500 index returned 2.12% in the US. The major stock indexes, in foreign countries did much better : Germany, 3.44%, Britan, 3.7%, France, 3.83% and Spain- 4.66% for example.

Another proverb is higher risk for higher returns. Higher risk many a times translated into higher losses also. While safe, low risk investment result into lower return, but also accord safety. Inflation, after taxes, are the biggest impediment to wealth creation. On average inflation has hovered around 3%, hence any kind of return that does not beat inflation, makes one loose value of their investments. If you earn 4% dividend or interest on your money, pay 1% in taxes you have left with 3% to put in your pocket. You just made zero % return on your investments, as inflation is 3%. If you put your money in checking, savings and CDs, and gain 0.5%, 1% and 2% return, after paying taxes you generated, -3%, -2.5% and -1% return on your money. If you feel good about FDIC protection, it means your money is insured to loose 1%-3% every year in FDIC protected accounts. Hence one has to beat inflation. If you do not, you will eventulaly loose your money over time, in safe investments.

There are 3 kinds of options : low-risk, medium-risk and high-risk. Interest in a low-risk dividend funds can genaret 3% return, you barely beat the 3% inflation, if you paid any taxes. In a medium-risk option, like real estate trust, one can generate 5% return with moderate risk, pay some taxes and still be ahedad of inflation, atleast by 1%. In a high-risk option one can buy some stocks and get 7-8% return and feel happy. But this does not hapen time and again, many year some losses, say of -10% to -15% also occur.

Dow jones was at 14,000 during 2004, and was at 7,000 during 2007, a loss of 50%, and is at 12,000 in 2016, still 10% lower than its peak in 2015, now 21,000. Talking about banking crisis, unemployment, real estate debacle, will make it even more depressing.

35

Insurance Rescue

Haven't you heard, 'buy term and invest the difference' ? Buy cheap term, put funds in stock market, and you will get better return than with permanent life plans. After age 65, you do not need life insurance, as your mortgage is paid, children are educated, you have collected enough in retirement funds.

But the truth is always far away. Biggest life policies are purchased after age 70, for hundreds of thousands of premiums, for estate conservation, and for tax-free pension. Billionaires can not get as much life insurance as they want, due to insurance industry regulations.

During the last 30 years, trillions of dollars of term insurance has been purchased. Most will lapse during the next 10-30 years. 99% of all term insurance lapses, and claims on them are never paid. These generate the biggest profits for the insurance industry. No wonder, most top ranked companies have stopped offering permanent, guaranteed, whole life policies. Even with high premiums these end up in huge claims and payments by the insurance companies.

Similarly, anticipating a huge influx of elderly people, in the coming decades, and obvious situations of paying for nursing home and home health care costs, most insurance companies have stopped offering, LTCI, long term care insurance. Hence, Whole Life, and LTCi, have become precious commodities. Do not loose , if you have them. Get as much as you can, of both, WLi and LTCi. Term insurance premiums, at the renewal time, increases 10x, ten fold, in premiums, and mostly lapse, or cancelled.

But Qualifying Insureds do not have to loose the policy, and do not have to loose all the premiums paid in the last 10-30 years or so. They may receive a cash payment for most of the premiums paid, in many cases more than they have paid. They can keep a reduced coverage for life, instead of asking for cash settlements, through Term Life Insurance Rescue Program.

Longer the policy has lasted, Older the client is, and more significant the health issues are, more funds are generated from those Term Insurance policies. Reduced policy values, without any future premium payments can also be arranged, if cash is not desired.

Insurance Trust

"If you earn a dollar, Uncle Sam may take as much as 41 cents, If you save a dollar, he may take as much as 55 cents." Seems unfair, doesn't it ?

This is what President Obama and Republicans are trying to tackle, these days, and the Democrats are working on making the issue more complicated. George Bush, gave us freedom from Estate Taxes, which expired in 2010. Whatever is going to be decided, nothing will be permanent, as Congress, has the hobby to change the rules again and again, and this is what they do to justify their existence.

Insurance Trust, ILIT, Irrevocable Life Insurance Trust is an important tool for Estate Planning, and saves on taxes.

Persons who, over their lifetimes, successfully accumulate an estate made up of cash, Real Estate (both developed and undeveloped), or a substantial interest in a closely held business, face one major problem someday, Called ESTATE SHRINKAGE. Starting at 35% and going up quickly to 55%, and even higher in some circumstances, the Federal Estate Tax can destroy a lifetime's efforts, especially if the estate is composed largely of illiquid assets such as real estate. In addition to Federal Estate Tax, the different States also levy, State Estate Tax. How do the affluent people plan on saving on Estate Taxes. Of course by proper Estate Planning.

Law and Internet : Bharara Brothers

Preet Bharara, US Attorney, NY has made quite a name (and money) for himself, cleaning Wall Street mess. He succeeded in 43 convictions, in the last 2 years, for insider trading. An excellent record.

Preet, 47, graduated from Harvard, and got his law degree from Columbia. He has been an Assistant US attorney, and chief counsel for Senator Chuck Schumer, D-NY.

His brother, Vinit Bharara, 44, graduated from University of Pennsylvania, and followed his brother to Columbia Law School. Vinit did practice law for a while but then he left to start an internet company, called Pit, a sports card trading company, later bought by Topps Co. Preet was skeptical about his brother's career move, and expected Vinit, to finally follow in his footsteps in Law.

While Preet has been chasing crooks on Wall Street, his brother Vinit, has hawked diapers on line. Few years ago, Vinit called Preet to say that he was going to sell diapers for a living. Preet said, Oh, really ? What, door to door ? Preet asked his brother. No, on the internet, his brother answered.

Lately, Preet was speaking to Wall Steet executives and narrated, Vinit had called, and asked, Hey, bro, how's that U.S. Attorney thing working out for you ? I just sold my company to Amazon for $540 million. Preet was stunned. There is a lot more money to be made cleaning up babies than cleaning up Wall Street. Preet is Professor in NY now.

Life Settlement

How do you settle a life insurance policy ? You sell it for a huge profit.

Any unwanted life policy can be sold, like any other property. Term policies do not have cash value, but they can be sold too. In permanent policies, there is always some cash value, selling such a policy will generate several times more funds than the cash surrender value of the policy.

Let us say you bought a policy to cover a loan, loan is repaid, or the property is sold, the policy is not needed any more. Do not cancel the policy, just sell it.

You needed a life policy for buy-sell agreement between 2 or more partners, the partnership is dissolved, policy has no use, instead of cashing the value, sell it for many more times of return. Longer the policy has remained in force, more money you get for it.

Divorce can create situations, where unnecessary policies can be sold to spouses or in the open market.

It could be the same, when a business partnership is dissolved.

Your policy premiums are increasing, and you feel unhappy paying those high premiums, it is getting unaffordable, sell the policy. You may try acquiring another lower premium policy. Just do not get rid of the old policy, since you can submit it to the settlement market for cash.

Life insurance companies love to see policies getting terminated, cancelled, or surrendered for cash, as they are no longer required, or obligated then to pay a huge death benefit at the end of the term, or when the insured, or owner dies. But there are a host of life settlement companies that do just the opposite. They buy unwanted policies, keep on paying premiums, and collect the huge death benefit at a future date. But they provide enough cash incentives to the owners of those policies, and purchase the ownership rights. Do not cancel a life policy, do not let it lapse, do not surrender it, but try to settle it.

39

Lincoln Lost Home

President Abraham Lincoln lost his homes twice. Lincoln was born in a one-room cabin in Hodgenville, KY. President's father Tom Lincoln had paid $200 for the cabin and 300 acres of adjoining piece of land.

It was a modest place, but was their home. After four years, Lincolns had to pack up and leave as there was a defect in title. Lincolns did not have the right kind of papers, and someone else had a better claim to the land. Abe, then three years old and in his mother's arms, the family moved eight miles away to Knob Creek.

Tom Lincoln, after a few years at the new place, had to go to the court to prove the ownership right to the second farm and their second home. Another claimant sued him as a 'tresspasser'. Tom Lincoln won the suit, but became fearful that he might someday loose his second home and property. People were talking about Land-titles, landowners, landlords, land laws, land-lawyers and land-sharks. He became unsure of his title, and thought that he might have 'the wrong kind of papers'. Tom finally moved away to Indiana, where there were plenty of Government Land with Clear Titles, and the right kinds of papers. Lincoln thus lost a second home to title problems.

We all have horror stories of these kinds from India, where things have not improved much.

Today title insurance is as important as ever. Both buyers and sellers should insist on procuring a title insurance at any real estate closing to avoid any title problems.

Longevity

In Sanskrit, they say, 'Jeevet Shardah Shatam'. Live for Hundred years. But the financial aspects of living longer, has other considerations too. Here is the saying, 'You will be around, but will your money ?'.

Your money has to last, until you do. People live longer now and retirement may last equal to working years. Hence the concern on adequate funds to survive till the end.

Here are some interesting facts on Longevity in the US.

Life Expectancy has kept on increasing, 1900s - 49 years, 1920 - 56, 1940 - 64, 1960 - 70, 1980 - 74, 2000 - 79. Women live 5 years longer than men. The average life expectancy for men now is 76, while 81 for women. After the age of 80 the ratio of widows to widowers is 5 to 1.

The highest life expectancy is in Hawaii, 81.5 years, and the lowest in Mississippi, 74.8, Georgia seems to do OK 77-78.

There are more centenarians in US now than ever before, a total of 53,000 people are over the age of 100. Everyday 10,000 people turn 65.

What makes us to live longer ?

Here are a few tips:

1. Be friendly and helpful to others, positive relationships help.

2. Get a pet, 12% more chance of surviving a heart attack if you have a pet.

3. Sleep enough, minimum of 4 hours, more than 8 hours reduces life expectancy.

4. Intimacy reduces stress, improves sleep quality, and bonds people (especially couples) together.

5. Optimistic, happy people avoid premature death, by 50%. Indulging in pity-party increases pessimism.

The value of exercise and meditation can never be overemphasized. Meditation relieves from Stress.

Physical activities enhance longevity, and maintain good health. One hour of exercise everyday extends life by 11 hours, while 2.5 hours of moderate activity per week can extend life expectancy by 4.5 years.

People in US save very little. Saving more for rainy days, for retirement, for long life is very important.

To make money last longer, one should consider the following:

Work longer, do not retire early, preferably to age 70.

Start saving today, time value of money is enormous, longer you do, better it gets.

Have a specific plan to accumulate enough funds, 10-20 times of annual salary needed for retirement.

Maximize social security benefits, instead of drawing benefits, wait until 70, which increases the pot much.

Keep plenty of insurance to avoid economic risks, and cover for life, medical, and long term care costs.

Long-Term-Care

Any one, at any age may require Long-Term-Care or Critical-Care, due to prolonged illness, birth defects, disability and old age. It is estimated that, by the year 2030, 8.5 million people will be over age 85 in the United States. Who is going to take care of these elderly people? In ancient cultures, the extended families stayed together and the younger members took care of the elderly. Civilization breaks the family bonds and people tend to live away from each other, across the globe for convenience, life-style, jobs and emoluments.

We often hear, 'world is a global village now' and 'just a click away'. But consider this. Me and my wife are living in Atlanta, and aging with grace, have qualified for Pension and Medicare. Our children live in Los Angeles and San Francisco in California with their spouses and children. If we are sick for extended periods, if we can not take care of ourselves due to old age, or are bed ridden, can our children fly in from California and take care of us, live with us for long periods, take us to keep us with them in their tiny condos near Hollywood ? Of course not. Some things never change, they are not 'just a click away', the geographical distances still matter. The happiest people in the world, in China, India and on African Continent and elsewhere still live within a few miles, surrounded with all their extended family members, whom they visit very often and seek from, and provide help to each other in times of need, including care of the elderly at hospice. Elderly people are respected and helped like babies, since they raised the next generation.

Due to this problem of old age and sickness, we find the growth of Nursing homes, and facilities to care for the aged.

Diseases of the brain and aging, Dementia and Alzheimers' further complicate the care of the elderly. Life insurance takes care of premature death, and may be used to pay for estate taxes and generate funding in old age. Long-Term-Disability Insurance takes care of lost income, for few years and generally stops at age 65, when people retire. Short-Term-Disability Insurance can reimburse one's income for periods from few weeks to few months. Medical Insurance pays for the expenses of sickness. Critical-Care Insurance helps for specific needs like for the care of cancer, stroke and heart attacks, or serious accidents.

But the value of Long-Term-Care Insurance is paramount. Everyone above the age of 50 must have it, though people at younger ages may need it too. There is an inevitable fact, that we all age. Many of us will live longer than we expected. Some of use will live too long. There will be 70 million people of age 65 and above in the US by 2030, and there will be 8.5 million of them above 85. Please buy your Long-Term-Care Insurance early, as cost and premiums increase to exorbitant levels at older ages. The sandwich generation, which is taking care of young children and is also struggling and worried about the care of their aging parents, need to buy Long-Term-Care Insurance on themselves, for future use, as well as on their parents (and may be on grand parents), so that the elderly can be served with dignity in a nursing home, and lodged in an eldercare facility. Caring for elderly is difficult. It consumes lots of time, and lots of funds, hence the LTCI, Long-Term-Care Insurance should come very handy.

Long-Term-Care financing is a vital part of Estate- and Financial-Planning, and should be seriously considered when planning for retirement. The high cost of extended stays in nursing home, and home health care by competent medical and paramedical personnel is very expensive. It is unwise not to have this, LTCI, coverage even if you have plenty of wealth, as funds deplete fast enough, and many people outlive their savings.

Long-Term-care Polices now come with many bells and whistles. They provide for all expenses needed for at home care of the elderly, disabled or mentally and physically challenged. They also provide for bed reservation and extended stay with medical help, meals, room and board etc at nursing homes. Some policies can be paid for in few years for a life time of coverage, and some refund your premium if you do not use it, while others will pay a huge death benefit, if you died prematurely without using the benefits of Long-Term-Care.

It is advised that one should invest plenty of funds in a good LTCI policy that can pay for care at home or in a institution, where there is need for it, refund you money when you need the money or do not need the benefits of the policy, and/ or pays benefits to your heirs like a life insurance policy does.

⊘

Love my 401(K)

Congratulations on contributing to the retirement partnership program, with your Employer and the Government, both Federal and State. Some of the highlights of the program :

You will be the sole contributor, Government will not put any funds into it, the Employer may help with a miniscule amount. If you leave the job early, the Employer Match will be returned to the Employer, called Vesting.

You will not be taxed on your contribution, disguised as Tax-Deduction.

We, the Government, will determine how much you can save, 25% of income, up to $18,000, for 2016.

You will bear all the expenses and fees, fund charges, management fee, reporting fee, and will take all the risks of the market.

You can not access the account until age 59½, unless you pay a penalty (10%) and taxes (25-33%), hence sending, us, 40% or so as our share, and we will let you have the rest 60%.

We, the Government, will determine what your share will be in future and will reserve the right to change our percentage, the taxes.

Between age 60 and 70, you can take as much as you like from the account, but have to pay ordinary income taxes, which will be much higher than you are paying now, 25-30%.

We will collect over 30%, as our share and let you have less than 70%, your share.

We, the Government, will decide how much you can take out from the age 70 onwards. But will collect 30% or so in taxes, and let you keep the rest, 70% or so.

If you take less, than we allow, or if you want to save for later, or for your heirs, we will charge a penalty of 50% and the tax, 33%, collect 83% as our, Government's, share and let you have the rest, 17%.

If you died, with retirement funds not distributed, we will charge 30% in taxes and 45% in estate taxes, and collect our share of 75%, and will let you have the rest 25%.

If you wish to put $10,000 a year, into your 401(K), we will help you save on taxes, say $3000, at 30%. When you are ready to retire, and have contributed $10,000 over 30 years or so, and put $10,000 x 30 years = $300,000 in the account, we have allowed, over $3000 x 30 years = $90,000 of tax savings. Because, we, the Government, are very generous to the public. However, when the account has grown from $300,000 to say $1,000,000 in the account in 30 years, we will be there to collect $300,000 in taxes, at 30%. We invested $90,000 in you and have patiently waited 30 years, hence we deserve to make at least $300,000. It seems very fair. We may collect more, to fund those wars and other expenses.

Please add your State Taxes, 6% in Georgia, to the above percentage(s) of Federal Taxes.

Good Luck, Please save more, in your 401(K).

During 1980s, annuity pensions were removed and replaced with 401K plans. Both by the Government and the Private Sector.

This revolution opened the flood gates, every one started investing in the stock market, which has created risky plans, without any guarantees.

Whom has it helped more, ordinary public or Wall Street guys? You decide. Wonder, why people are occupying Wall Street? Again, 20 years later, during 2000s, the Government tried hard to put all the money people pay in Social Security Taxes, into Stock Market, but did not succeed. Social Security stayed as Annuity, where payments are guaranteed for life. Congress kept the social security deposit out of the markets. However, other financial measures, created the cliff of 2007-2008, worse than that of the depression of 1930s. Any surprise, why 90% people are poor in the US ?

MyRA

In Jan 2014, in the State of the Union address, President Obama explained the new retirement plan, called myRA, or my retirement account . This was followed by the presidential memo, asking the Department of Treasurey to create a new kind of retirement funding. This was done without any approval from the Congress, just by an executive order form the President.

This has been done to help middle and lower income workers to set up retirement account, even if their employers do not offer a retirement plan. The white house is encouraging the Employers to offer, myRA through payroll deduction. There is no employer matching, common in the regular 401(K) plans, and the employees can contribute, over and above the 401(K) plan, if one already exists, if they earn less than $191K of household income, a year.

The account will function like a Roth IRA, the funds will be invested after-tax, hence there is no tax deduction as in traditional IRA, but the funds are distributed tax-free, as in Roth IRA. However, unlike any other retirement plans, the funds will be invested in government savings bonds only, will earn a descent rate of return, now around 2%, will avoid stock market risks, and has no fees. President's proposal for automatic enrollment of employees in the plan will require congressional approval.

The minimum contribution of $5-$25 a month is allowed, but when the account reaches the amount of $15K, or has been open for 30 years, it would automatically convert into a Roth IRA. Withdrawals from the myRA accounts are permitted anytime, but any gains may be taxable before age 59 ½. The accounts will be portable and can move from one employer to another.

There is a retirement savings crisis in our country, but this one, the myRA, will not solve the problem much. It can be said that it is too little, and too late. But something is always better than nothing.

No/Yes, Life Insurance

Insurance a necessary evil. With so many kinds, we need to acquire, car, home, biz, liability, medical, dental, vision, disability, long term care, life, malpractice etc, it may seem so. But that is not true. Insurance is a social device, where members put a small portion of their funds in a common pool, called premium, and expect to get a bigger amount paid, called claim at the time of loss. Insurance companies that collect premiums and pay claims are allowed to keep only 2% of the premiums collected for their administrative functions, hence they have to raise premiums so often. Most often the profits are returned back to the public as dividends, which is normally return of premium, and non-taxable.

The most dreaded is life insurance, which no one wants to buy. Which industry, has most sales people working for ? The answer, Insurance. Which product is sold most ? Again, Insurance. Which kind of sales people make the highest income ? The insurance Agents, especially the life insurance agents.

Why then people are not buying life insurance ? Due to the hype on investing in stock market, which Makes those 99% poor, and occupy the Wall Street.

People say they do not have NEED for life insurance. But Life insurance has to be purchased When you do not need it. When you need it you can not get it. People do not have MONEY to buy it. Life Insurance is bought with good health and is paid for by money, premium. It is a necessary evil, 8-10% of gross income must be spent to buy insurance, to protect economic losses. People are not in HURRY to buy insurance. But they have to be in hurry. Your health can change overnight, you can get killed or become disabled in an accident, anytime. Procrastination and not being prudent creates biggest of disasters.

Buy as much life insurance as you can. INFLATION, will erode its value over time, and you may not qualify to get more at a lower rate in future. Just hurry to put it in force. Term insurance, temporary, the cheap stuff, is the most expensive way to buy insurance, 97% get cancelled and never have claims. Permanent is expensive, but 100% result into claims, and those cost lots of funds to the insurance company, much more than they charge in premiums. Hence the high premium. Who are the biggest life insurance purchasers ? The Banks. They bring millions and billions of dollar to insurance companies to buy whole life insurance. They get 6-7% tax-deferred dividends, tax-free death benefits at pennies for dollars. Insurance companies always avoid issuing those big policies for banks, not taking too much risk, and be liquid for the small policy owners.

This story will illustrate the significance of life insurance.

Few Horsemen in the night were stopped by a strange voice. "Please dismount and collect as much pebbles as you can in your pockets and then proceed." They did, but collected only few pebbles, in their pockets, since their pockets were getting full, and it was becoming heavy.

In the morning they found out that those pebbles were diamonds. They were sorry not to collect more pebbles, but were happy that they did some. More life insurance you buy, happier you will be.

(45)

Obamacare / Trumpcare

Obamacare began Jan 1, 2014, and the Healthcare Exchanges, now called Marketplace, began Oct 1, 2013. 40 states have started their own Exchanges, while the other 10 will have mandatory Federal Exchanges.

There would be no pre-existing conditions clause, all will be accepted. Coverage will be unlimited, there will be no life time caps.

To cover older and sicker people, everyone, including young and healthy must purchase health insurance, or pay a penalty of $100, which increases to $695 by the year 2016.

This Individual Mandate was implemented by IRS, from Jan 1, 2014.

Employers must offer and provide medical insurance to all employees, or pay a fine of $166 per employee per month, or $2000 per year. The Employer mandate was delayed until Jan 1, 2015. Unemployed and low income people will receive subsidy to buy insurance, and must procure from State Exchanges.

Younger and healthier people may have to pay higher premium, to generate funds for older and sicker people to obtain affordable coverage.

Private insurers like Blue Cross, Kaiser, Aetna, Humana, Unitedhealthcare, Assurant, Nippon, Cigna and others, will offer policies based on the guidelines from State and Federal marketplace. The 2 websites to navigate for further information are : www.nahu.org and www.ehealthinsurance.com.

Subsidy will be available for people making less than $46K for single, and $94K for a family. Subsidy for a family will be around $6700 per year to purchase medical insurance, based upon 9.5% of the adjusted gross family income of $70,650. Paying for COBRA will not qualify for subsidy.

People who get insurance through their employers, will not see much change, except there will be more generous coverage, of course at higher premiums. Younger and healthy may pay more, while older and sick will pay less.

State and Federal Exchanges, now known as marketplace, will have many kinds of plans, Platinum, Gold, Silver and Bronze and catastrophic policy for people under 30. Further information should be available at www.healthcare.gov. COBRA will still be available, will not qualify for subsidy, but better deals may be found out of government exchanges, run by private insurers.

Trumpcare, is, AHCA, American Health Care Act, compared to Obamacare, ACA, Affordable Care Act. It is in the making for the last 10 years and the full implications will be known in the next 10-20 years, by then, we may have Medicare for All. Premiums will reduce, mandates will be removed, and the coverages will be diluted. Insurers will participate fully in the business of healthcare. Individuals and Employers may get relief due to lower taxes and lack of fines. Medical insurance will revert to the situation, as it was before the ACA began, and there may be several versions of healthcare and different levels of premiums, in different areas, and in different states of the Union.

Optimizing Distributions

One of the most important financial decisions that many individuals will have to make in the coming years is one that few pepole have actually planned for. It is a decision that will have a critical impact not only on their own financial security but also on the financial well-being of their children and grandchildren. It is a decision that may seem simple at first, but is really quite complex. In fact, many accountants, stockbrokers, attorneys, and financial advisors are unaware of the importance and complexity of this decision.

This decision is how to structure the distributions from their "traditional" IRAs (Roth IRAs have different distribution rules) to meet their retirement needs and to maximize their family's wealth.

Individuals must make three important and complicated decisions for their IRA distributions. First, they must decide when to begin distributions: second. they must name beneficiaries to the account; finally, they must choose a life expectancy calculation method.

The Internal Revenue Service requires individuals to begin taking distributions from their IRAs by April of the calendar year follwoing the year in which they turn 70½ (the Required Beginning Date). Withdrawals can begin before 70½ but there may be a 10% penalty on distributions before the age of 59½.

Naming a beneficiary to an IRA is important first because the IRA assets are distributed directly to the named beneficiaries on the account after the death of the IRA owner. Selection of a beneficary for an IRA is equally important because it impacts the minimum distributions that the IRA owner must take each year while alive.

Once the Required Beginning Date arrives, the IRS requires IRA owners to take minimum withdrawals each year from their accounts. This minimum withdrawal - called the Minimum Required Distribution (MRD) is calculated by dividing the amount in the IRA by the applicable life expectancy. If a beneficiary is named to an IRA, then the owner may use a joint life expectancy - with some restrictions- to calculate the MRDs. By naming a beneficiary to the IRA, then, the owner can reduce the amount of the MRDs, allowing more money to remain in the IRA to compund tax-dererred. Naming a beneficiary to the IRA may also allow the beneficiary to continue receiving the MRDs after the owner's death based on the beneficiary's life expectancy.

Many people also don't realize that assets in their IRAs will be included in their taxable estates when they die. Rather than deplete the IRA assets to pay the applicable estate taxes, they may want to use other, non-retirement assets to pay the taxes. A qualified financial advisor can illustrate creative and tax-effeient ways to use life insurance and other investment products to pay these taxes.

The foregoing material only begins to describe the complexity of planning IRA distributions. The choices that are made may result in very different financial results for individuals and their families. The wrong choices may mean financial disaster; the right choices may mean financial security for generations.

Pension Plan Limits

At the end of the year. Individuals have their W2, 401(K) and other statements, and contemplate on adding funds to their retirement accounts, like IRA, individual retirement arrangements, Full, $5,500, or catch up $6,500 for those over age 50, or non-deductible Roth-IRA.

Employer sponsored 401(K) can accommodate up to $18,000.

Filling for the 1040 tax returns by April 15th for the individuals is required. Business owners are busy preparing the balance sheet, profit and loss statements, and putting funds in Corporate Retirement Plans, and filing tax returns through IRS form 1120 by March 15, for the last tax year. Extensions are allowed.

Contribution limit for Simple-IRA, remains at $12,00, and the catch up at $2,500.

But Employers, with high incomes need bigger contributions in the pension plans, especially those who plan to retire early.

Self employed individuals can set up, SEP-IRA, simplified employee pension-ira, which allows $52K in contributions, and is tax deductible to the corporation. The same is true of specific 401(K) plans, where employees receive higher contribution from employers and have immediate vesting, that allows $52K in contributions, under safe harbor rules.

Defined Contribution, DC, plan under IRC, internal revenue code, 415, also allows contributions of $52K.

The biggest deduction can be taken through, IRC 412, $210K, called a defined benefit, DB, plan.

The definition of Highly Compensated Employee under IRC 414 has remained at $115K of compensation, will continue at this level, for social security contribution and deduction purposes.

But a Key Employee Officer under IRC 416, with compensation of $165K is increasing to $170K.

In addition to all this, the non-deductible, retirement contribution, sometimes called as Bonus or SERP, supplemental employee retirement plan, can be funded with unlimited amounts and is purely discriminatory.

It is discretionary, and is not guided by any rules of IRS, internal revenue service, and DOL, department of labor. It is also exempt from ERISA, employees retirement security act, hence called PPP, Private Pension Plan.

Most retirement plans that are funded through tax-deductible contributions, like, IRA, SEP, 401(K), 403(b), 457, 415, 412, distribute proceeds as ordinary income and are taxable as such, in retirement. These Retirement benefits have 10% penalty, if withdrawn before age 59 ½, and have 50% penalty if NOT withdrawn after age 70 ½, as RMD, required minimum distribution, in addition to ordinary income taxes.

The Roths, and SERPs, where contributions are non-deductible, are exempt from any income taxes when distributed and do not have to follow the pre-59 ½ and post-70 ½ rules, and in most cases make better Pension benefits.

PPACA

Patient Protection and Affordable Care Act

PPACA, Patient Protection and Affordable Care Act is commonly known as Obamacare. It came in a big way. Healthcare Exchanges were created, to provide medical, dental benefits to the public. These exchanges will be created by Private Insurers, as Private Exchanges, while those created by the Government, both Federal and State, will be known as Government Exchanges. Benefits offered are going to be huge and generous, like no restrictions for pre-existing conditions, and unlimited benefits. However, to cut costs and waste, there will be emphasis on streamlining the benefits. Exchanges are expected to create competition and lower prices, premiums.

However, some of the things are obvious. Healthy consumers will pay much higher premium, while sicker consumers will pay less. Because healthy people will subsidize the cost of insurance for sicker people.

People with chronic illness will be able to afford the insurance at reasonably lower cost. People who do not have insurance, will be mandated to purchase the coverage or pay a fine to IRS, as an added tax. Large Employers, have to offer insurance benefits to their employees or pay a fine of $2000 per employee. But the Obama Administration has decided, temporarily, not to impose those fines on the employers. Smaller Employers will get a subsidy from the government to buy insurance for their employees. Some people hope that individual mandates may also be not implemented for the time being. It will definitely be a while, when the full impact of the new law will be realized.

All this is coupled with Medicare, Medicaid and the Food Stamp Program for the poor and needy. The Food Stamp Program, administered by the US Department of Agriculture, is proud to be distributing this year the greatest amount of free meals and food stamps ever, to 47 Million people.

Meanwhile, the National Park Service, administered by the US department of the Interior, asks us, "Please Do not feed the animals." Their stated reason for the policy, "The animals will grow dependent on handouts and will not learn to take care of themselves."

49

Pre-and Post-nups

The acronyms stand for Prenuptial- and Postnupital- Agreements, made prior to a wedding and when a marriage is in trouble. Remember, who sang, 'Baby, you are a Rich Man'. Of course, Beatle Paul McCartney.

His marriage few years ago cost $3.2 Million. The couple are up for divorce, which is expected to get Heather Mills up to $375 Million.

Over fifty percent of marriages in the USA evaporate in divorce, and 'till death do us apart' no longer holds good. Marriages are made in heavens, and having same spouses in previous and future births, believed in by some, have become matters of ridicule.

Even in the lives of people from Indian Subcontinent, famous for 'everlasting marriages', 'eternal bliss', 'everlasting love', and 'happily ever after...' is disppearing fast.

Prenuptial agreements are getting their day due to the break of marriages of British Royalty, Hollywood and Bollywood Couples, and many not so publicized marriages between people of lesser financial worth. Let us hope Imran Khan and Arun Nayar have their prenups in place. The agreement may seem unromantic, but should be a means to Happy marriage, and avoid a nasty divorce.

Both Death and Divorce, put assets to similar risks. We prepare a 'Will' to settle our 'Estates', after we are gone, death being certain, and their heirs save a lot of heartache, knowing what they expect to inherit, and avoid lengthy legal battles. Marriages, lasting less than a lifetime, or say less than a decade now, need Prenups to keep spouses and their children sane, during marriages and also when it is terminated. Whether one has substantial assets prior to marriage, especially in late and second (and latter) marriages.

It is said that, 'divorcing without a prenup is like dying without a will'. Even people of modest means, have different values about 'money' (regarding, how to spend or save it) and accumulate assets fast, and may end up with a 'nasty divorce'. Without specific instructions, due to the lack of a 'Will' and 'Prenups' courts apply their own reasoning for dividing the assets between heirs and spouses.

After the romance fades, and the realities of the fragile and selfish relationships set in, a Prenuptial agreement should go a long way to save the marriage or terminate it with less heartache. Even Postnuptial agreement, when differences erupt in marriages, and couples are still on speking terms (may be still living together), can be used to settle marital and financial issues, and mnch of 'he said/did', and 'she said/did' can be avoided.

Postnups generally have higher standards of fairness than Prenups should be obvious.

But the legal strengths of Postnups is weaker than the Prenups, since spouses may be coerced into undesirable Postnup settlements to get out of the relationship faster, than cancelling the wedding, and not getting into an unfair Prenup. For both prenup and postnup to work effectively, two separate counsels should be used for the two parties.

With all it complicated ramifications, it is time, people from the Eastern World, especially Indian Subcoritinent, of all religious callings, consider prenups seriously, the details of which can be discussed with legal-practitioners and financial-planners who specialize in the subject.

50

Premium Financing

If you earn a dollar, Uncle Sam may take as much as 41 cents.

If you save a dollar, he may take as much as 55 cents.

Seems unfair, doesn't it ?

41 cents comes from income taxes, on earnings, 35% for federal and 6% for state.

55 cents comes form estate taxes, due after death, from the assets left.

Protection of assets can be achieved by leveraging credit, which is an efficient way to insure the wealth.

This strategy is also known as Leveraged Funding or Premium Financing.

Premium Financing is an option for high net worth individuals who need additional insurance for the purpose of saving on estate taxes, but do not want to pay for it. They do not want to reduce their cash flow, or even do not want to liquidate their assets to pay for premium payments.

This situation requires the use of borrowed funds from a commercial lender to pay for insurance premiums and has several advantages:

Minimizes the gift and estate taxes, or completely eliminates them, helps keep other assets intact, and makes them grow further.

Can preserve the Unified credit, up to $11 Million.

To accomplish premium financing certain steps need to be taken with help from an accountant, CPA and a estate planning, tax attorney. Finally a financial planner should be able to put all the pieces together for smooth functioning of the plan.

1. Establish an ILIT, irrevocable life insurance trust, and fund the trust.

2. Obtain a Life Policy, and close the loan from a financial institution, that acts as an Alliance.

3. Premium Finance the Loan and set up collateral arrangement.

4. Gift enough funds, cash to the ILIT.

5. Establish a GRAT, Grantor Retained Annuity Trust, to repay the loan.

6. Repayment of the Loan, is done most of the times from the cash value of the Life policy.

7. ILIT receives the death proceeds of the policy, and disburses proceeds to the Heirs, tax-free.

A 10 pay whole life, with increasing term rider to generate maximum death benefit works best in this situation., and generates huge amounts of tax-free wealth for future generations.

51

QDT, Qualified Domestic Trust

Legisiation known as "TAMRA" has quickly, but quite effectively, eliminated the estate and gift tax marital deductions for property passing to a spouse who is not a citizen of the United States. Although propertis passing to a spousee on a tax-free or tax-deffered basis, these changes have caused problems that can be solved only through estate planning and the use of life insurance. The planning sould be accomplished through professionals familiar with tax law.

The IRS Code disallows the estate tax marital deduction for property passing to a non-citizen spouse, resident or non-resident, except where the property passes in a qualifie Domestic Trust." (A QDT is a trust in which the trustee is required to be a U.S. citizen or domestic corporation, the surviving spouse is entitled to all the income payable at least annually, and with respect to which the deceased is executor and has made an election on the estate tax return. There are a number of provision that make QDT significantly different from most trusts :

1. Probate and non-probate property can be transferred to the QDT by the surviving spouse within 9 months of the deccased's death. Probate property not transferred to a QDT cannot qualify for the marital deduction.

2. Any distribution of QDT corpus to the surviving spouse, and all remaining QDT assets at the death of the spouse, are taxed as though included in the estate of the first spouse to die. In other words, the advantage of graduated estate tax rates for two spouses is seriously reduced.

3. A maximum of $100,000 can be transferred annually to a non-citizen spouse outright and pass free of gift tax.

When a property is owned jointly, (the surviving spouse being a non-citizen), the jointly held property is treated as owned in proportion to the contributions made by each spouse for the purchase of the property. The following is a hypothetical example, Prakash and Rita Misra own a home valued at $300,000. The house was purchased 10 years ago with funds furnished 90% by Prakash. (Rita does not work outside the home.) If Prakash dies and Rita is a U.S. citizen, $150,000 or 50% of fair market value, will be includible in Prakash's estate. On the other hand. If Rita is not U.S. citizen, $270,000 (90%) will be includible in Prakash's estate. Therefore, estate taxes of $77,600 are due the IRS at Prakash's death, (assuming Prakash owned nothing else and the couple has already used the unified credit of $600,000). This example applies to any asset owned by the couple.

These new provisions means that every couple, at least one of whom lacks U.S. citizenship, must review their estate plans. The following are some issues to consider.

A QDT does not avoid death taxes it only defers them until the death of the 2nd spouse. A tailored life insurance plan will pay these taxes for pennies on the dollar.

Any property which is intended to pass outright to the non US citizen spouse will be taxed, or erode the unified credit, unless a gifting program is implemented (maximum $100,000.00). The $ 600,000 unified credit is not available to "non-resident" aliens, which now stands at $5.5 Million.

Any non-probate property will undergo similar treatment except for postmortem opportunity to transfer such property to a QDT.

All Trusts, testamentary or living trusts, the value of which is includable in the deceased spouse's estate must meet QDT requirements if the marital deduction is to be available.

But all QDT corpus is ultimately taxed as though it were part of the estate of the first spouse to die, the surviving spouse's unified credit is unavailable to shelter this property from estate tax, unless the surviving spouse has sufficient additional property to apply toward her unified credit, part or all of that unified credit may be wasted.

The effect of the legislation will likely be that some estate taxes will be payable at the first death and that higher taxes will be due at the second death than would have been the case before TAMRA. Life Insurance placed outside the taxable estate will be needed to create additional liquidity and to defray the additional cost.

Life insurance placed outside the first deceased's estate will be the most attractive way of passing wealth outright to the non-U.S. Citizen spouse, since it will tirgger neither estate tax, income tax or gift tax nor erode the unified credit amount.

(52)

Real Estate

Buying a home to live in, is the best investment one can make in real estate, due to the tax incentives, pride of ownership and enjoyment. Many people are not ready for home ownership, as it brings some responsibilities along. Repairs, cost of utilities, maintenance of the yard and other things appear chores to many of us. Many a times if you do not itemize your expenses, getting home mortgage deduction may not be possible. Living in an apartment, is said to be, 'money down the drain', but many of us prefer to have fewer financial and home-maintenance responsibilities, and find renting easier and more attractive. However, there are hosts of reasons, homeownership is one of the most attractive financial propositions, one should fall for, as quickly as possible.

Once, someone has acquired a home as primary residence, he or she may want to invest further in real estate.

Buying further residential units can be done for rental income, vacation home and for similar purposes. Single family homes appreciate more than condominiums and town homes. But all of them have their own place in real estate market, especially the high-rise condo units in urban areas.

People also look for investing in commercial real estate, which requires bigger amounts of funds and complicated management skills. Many a times people get together, form partnerships, pool their resources and buy high value commercial projects. This could be from simple office condominiums (for personal use or for rental income), as well as strip shopping centers for 10,000 to 20,000 square feet of space with 5 or 6 shops to larger multilevel units that have offices on upper floor(s), and retail shops at the bottom. Many a times an an-

Invest & Insure (124)

chor, like a big grocery store (or movie theater) is required to be the in the middle of the complex to attract prospects for the ancillary businesses around like a hair salon, a pet store, a coffee franchise etc. Bigger and mega malls are all around the town, having several anchors and numerous ancillary stores, with huge parking lots to cater to the needs of thousands of shoppers at one place, and make available any kind of stuff people look for, from automobile dealerships to hotels, to restaurants and clothing stores, shoe shops and the like, all together as part of a conglomerate.

Investing in commercial real estate has its rewards, as it generates huge cash flow for those who succeed but proves to be a headache for those who don't. It takes lot of time to build wealth in real estate, and quick returns, especially in the US, and very diffcult to achieve. Pressure of human population, and availability of developed real estate are the two main factors determining the upward escalation of real estate value.

Buying and holding land for selling at a later date for huge profits is very speculative. It has big risks, but also has great potential of profit. No risk no reward, works in obvious ways in real estate. Land is a rare commodity, people and nations want more and more of it, pay very high price for land, and go through arduous processes (including fights and wars) to obtain more land and control it.

Investing in real estate on a modest scale, like owning ones' own home, and huge deals like buying hotels, office buildings, skyscrapers, all have their place in a real estate portfolio. No wonder, Real-Wealth comes from Real-Estate.

53

Retirement Planning

Last several years of recession, job losses, melt-down of real estate and banking, and the related economic problems the world over, has put retirement planning for business owners on back burner. People are working longer, not retiring and generally have no funds to place in retirement accounts. But planning for retirement must begin at age 18, when one starts the first job. 10% of earnings must be kept in an account for rainy days and emergencies. And 15% of gross income must be sheltered for retirement, since retirement (65-95+, 30 years or more) may last as long as working years (25-65, 40 years).

Inflation will increase the cost of goods and services, to much higher levels in the coming decades, hence one will need astronomical amounts of funds for retirement. People have become more conscious of retirement planning, due to economic uncertainties. The end of the year, when things tend to slow down is the best period to reflect upon retirement.

Six specific attitudinal and behavioral stages that occur, before and during retirement have been recently identified, through extensive surveys.

1. Imagination. 10 to 15 years before retirement, most people feel uneasy, but some feel happy and enthusiastic about retirement, as they still have some time left to recover from their losses.

2. Hesitation. 5 to 7 years before retirement, people start feeling secure about retirement, most have saved funds in employer sponsored plans, and on their own.

3. Anticipation. 1 to 2 years before retirement, people feel excited and look favorably towards retirement as they have made up their mind on what to do in retirement.

4. Realization. 1 or 2 years following retirement, the sense of 'liberation' is slowly overtaken by realities of retirement, and people feel 'forced into retirement'.

5. Reorientation. 5 to 10 years after retirement, people feel happier and 'on track' in accomplishing their goals, and most work with a financial advisor, to let their savings stretch further.

6. Reconciliation. 15 to 20 years after retirement, people experience depression, are troubled by loss of income, loss of social connections, and do not enjoy retirement much.

Whereever you are, in the above six phases, or even earlier, in your life cycle, say 20 to 25 years before retirement, plan for Retirement meticulously, through several plans offered by employer, like 401(K), 403(b), SEP, Roth, Simple, and/or on your own. Self-employed people can accomplish things much faster than those who work for others.

54

Reverse Mortgage

As the name implies, Reverse Mortgage, is opposite to a regular mortgage, where you let the equity in your home be taken over by a financial institution, which pays you a monthly income for life and receives the title (ownership) of the home after you are gone.

Reverse Mortgage is a smart way to generate a retirement income, from primary residence, for elderly people, normally above age 62, whose heirs may have no use of the residence, when the parents/grandparents expire, and the elderly people can free up their cash in their homes and enhance the quality of their lives with added financial help. It is a government insured program that provides cash, monthly income, and line of credit, all or one of these, (subject to HUD, Housing and Urban Development, lending limits) for a fixed term as long as one lives in their homes.

FHA, Federal Housing Authority has a program called, HCEM, Home Equity Conversion Mortgage. Fannie Mae has a, government sponsored program, called Home Keeper, that provides cash, line of credit or monthly income, subject to Fannie Mae lending limits for a fixed term or as long as you live in your home.

Several private financial institutions also provide Reverse Mortgage with even better terms than the government can provide. In all such cases, one gets a lump sum cash or regular monthly income, which one does not have to pay back, and one can still live in their homes, and own it.

To obtain a Reverse Mortgage, no income or credit verfication are required. The loan is automatically re-paid, after permanent move out from the home. Repayment never exceeds the value of the home. The cash advances are based on the borrower's age, value of the home, and the ability to access all the equity since the home was built. All the loans and payments to homeowners are tax-free.

Qualifying for a Reverse Mortgage, one has to be 62 or older, the home should be completely or almost completely paid for, and the home will eventually be acquired by the financial institution, that provided the income to the home-owner.

Once the children and grandchildren move away, build their own nests, have no use of your home, it is useful to think of Reverse Mortgage and utilize the inactive cash for your own needs, and spare your heirs, the hassles of real estate transaction, after you are gone.

(55)

Roth IRA

Due to tax-free earnings and flexible withdrawal options, Roth IRA is one of the most attractive retirement products available to the tax-payer.

The Roth Individual Retirement Arrangements enable one to accumulate funds on a tax-free basis and withdraw them (both principal and earnings) tax-free. Unlike the Traditional IRA, contributions to a Roth IRA are not tax-deductible. Hence the 'qualified distributions', from a Roth Account are tax-free.

Eligibility to contribute to Roth IRA depends on, a) having earned income, and b) adjusted gross income being within certain limits. Single tax-payers can contribute fully to Roth IRA, if their income are under $100,000. They may also contribute partially for incomes up to $120,000, after which the higher income earners become ineligible to contribute. The income limits for married filing joint, is higher at $160,000 for full contribution, and $190,000 for partial contribution, after which they become ineligible. Married filing separately can never contribute fully, and become ineligible after their income reaches $10,000 a year.

The annual contribution is limited at $5500 for each tax-payer until age 50. Older people can contribute up to $6500 per person, provided each spouse has earned income of at least the amount they contribute into Roth. Prior year contribution can be made until the tax-filing deadline of April 15th. Assets may be rolled over or transferred from one Roth IRA account to another. Other retirement plan assets like that of SEP IRA, Simple IRA, 403(b) etc can be rolled over or converted to Roth IRA by paying the taxes due. Distribution of assets from a Roth IRA account can be made anytime. But a 'qualified distribution', which is tax-free (again, both principal and earnings) are allowed after the account has existed for at least five years, participant has reached age 59 and ½, account owner has died or has become disabled, or uses the funds for the first time home buying expenses of up to $10,000. Roth withdrawals in 'non-qualified' ways are subject to (federal and state) income taxes and may also be subject to a 10% penalty.

Converting other retirement plans into non-taxable Roth IRA is of great importance. Roth IRA withdrawals are tax-free, and there is no mandatory minimum distribution requirement at age 70 and ½. Since the funds in a Roth account can be held indefinitely, the Government allows the conversion of regular pension/retirement funds to Roth IRA accounts to avoid the minimum distribution, by paying the income taxes in advance. But this conversion should be done with competent professional help, to avoid the pitfalls, and minimize the tax burden.

Converting Roth-IRA to Traditional is called Re-Characterization.

Roth Revolution

Roth-IRA is an excellent tool for retirement. Many a times it does not make sense to push funds in a employer sponsored, 401(K), 403(b) and other similar arrangements. Employers, most of the time, match a portion of the employee contribution, into the retirement plan(s) and it is prudent to take advantage of the matching, as it helps generate more funds for retirement faster. But there is always a catch. Employers will not match the full contribution one makes or is allowed to make by the government, IRS, for tax-deductible purposes. They generally match, 3% of the employers gross contribution, which comes to pittance.

Employees feel happy, getting a retirement plan started, decrease the taxes, and increase their take home pay, and eventually a lower W2 at year end. A lower W2 also creates an opportunity for employers to contribute less for FICA, FUTA and Social Security taxes. Employers thus match a little and save a lot, and also create the huge industry for stock brokers, and investment advisors.

It is, thus, advisable that employees contribute only the amount that is being fully matched, by their employer, in the corporate retirement plan. The rest of the funds, even if not tax-deductible should go into other vehicles. The loss of tax-deductibility, is also a gain in taxes, which become due when the funds are distributed, at retirement. The Government with the lure of tax-deductibility and tax-deferred growth, entices the public to invest more and more funds for retirement savings. But also builds its own treasury, by restricting, any withdrawals, before age 59 ½, with 10% penalty and 50% penalty for nonwrithdnewal, due to RMD after age 70 and ½. During the accumulation phase the funds, are tax-deductible and grow tax-deferred, but are distributed voluntarily after age 60, and mandatory after age 71, called RMD, required minimum distribution, based on ones' life expectancy, and taxed as ordinary income.

The tax savings during the accumulation phase are so small, and the tax payments at distribution are so large that most common retirement plans, make people poor, when they need the money most. Combined with inflation and the time value of money, all those fancy plans, 401(K), 403(b), SEP, Simple-IRA, Profit Sharing Plans, are of little help. Hence there is a false assumption that one will be in lower tax-bracket at retirement. Roth IRA with its non-deductibility during accumulation, and non-taxability during distribution defies those options of qualified plans, and comes out far ahead. Both those features, tax-free distributions, and no required minimum distribution, makes it unique. But there is another catch, in the form of income limitations, to be eligible to contribute to Roth accounts, $105K for single individuals and $166K for married filing joint. The contribution limits are $5500 for each participant, and $6500 for those above the age of 50, called catch up contribution.

If one is not eligible for Roth contributions, they can still contribute to the traditional IRAs, as tax-deductible contribution if there be no retirement plan with employer, or non-deductible contribution, without any income limitations. In addition, there is a provision of Roth 401(K), with an employer offering 401(K) contributions, made pre-tax. There is also a Roth conversion opportunity, where taxable IRAs can be converted to tax-free Roth IRA, by paying tax now and eventually save on higher taxes that will be due at maturity of the account. Due to loss of huge amounts in stock market, people are trying for a re-characterization of their Roth accounts, which has created some confusion to the whole situation. The last equation to the array of retirement plans is PLI, permanent life insurance. Not universal, not index, not variable, but only whole life, that generates more funds than Roth, and creates legacy and wealth.

Rule 219

Do retired couple cook more at home, or eat outside ? It depends. But they eat more outside, due to frequent travels and availability of retirement income from different sources.

If they paid just $5, excluding tax and gratuity, for each of their 3 daily meals for 365 days, they will pay a total of $219,000 at the end of 20 years.

$5 x 2 x 3 x 365 x 20 = $219,000.

If their budget allowed only $5 per meal, dining experience during retirement, needs rethinking. A $15 or $20 per meal, will cost $657,000 and $876,000 by 20th year.

This unfunded deficit amounts to $6.6 Trillion, as determined by Center for Retirement, Boston College (WWW.CRR.BC.EDU), which is unrelated to deficits in Social Security or the Federal Government.

There are several unknown funding deficits in the US, that need to be addressed when planning for retirement.

A financial professional can help generate higher guaranteed life-time income. The retirement income gap, based on necessary-expenses and comfort-expenses should be addressed with urgency. Maximizing contributions into IRA, Roth, 401(K), catch-up additions for age 50 and older should be of big help. Taking advantage of mortality credits, and the use of longevity formulas to set up guaranteed income streams will alleviate most of the pitfalls.

It will be useful to remember the statistics :

50% chance of one spouse surviving to age 92

25% chance of one spouse surviving to age 97

This road could be longer, and more difficult than the working years from age 30 through age 65.

Hence the phase of accumulation, and growth of funds, during the working years through savings and investments should be very differently treated than, the phase of withdrawing funds form a retirement portfolio. The games of accumulation and distribution change so drastically, that it needs prudence and expertise to manage a long retirement.

58

Saving Taxes

April 15th is looming close. Even if you take an extension, it may be helpful to learn of these tips.

Corporate taxes are due on March 15th, but extensions for several months can be obtained.

Get in touch with your accountant and CPA to save on taxes, as much as you can.

Please use the following facts to plan and execute a successful tax-savings strategy:

1. Bought a home? Tax credit (not deduction on income) of $8000 is available for first time home buyers. If bought a home after Nov 6, 2009, and still had a home, you can get a tax credit of $6,5000, worth 10% of the purchase price, not to exceed $6,500. This help will continue, Income limit $225,000.

2. Had a child in College ? You can claim $2,500 per student per year for four years of college, in addition to lifetime Learning Credit of $2,000 per year for improving skills. Income limit $160,000.

3. Bought a car ? You can deduct the sales taxes up to $49,500 of vehicle's price. Income limit $250,000.

4. Were Unemployed ? You can have first $2,400 of unemployment income tax-free. If both spouses were unemployed, one can claim $4,800. Expenses for finding a new job is deductible up to 2% of AGI, Adjusted Gross Income, as in previous years.

5. Spent on Medical Expenses ? You can deduct 7.5% of AGI,

as in previous years, but there may be more helps this year if you were on COBRA and paid for it.

6. Gave to Charity ? Helped poor and needy, in Earthquake, Sunami and other disasters? Any expenses can be deducted on tax return, 1040.

7. Lost Investing ? You can use up to $3000 in losses from stock market and similar investments. Any further losses can be carried over to next year.

8. Affected by Disasters ? Numerous federal disasters were declared. If the losses were above 10% of AGI, you can deduct them from income. Event for Previous years, the losses can be deducted if an amended return is filed.

9. Made Energy Efficient Home Improvements ? A credit worth of 30% of the cost of energy saving devices, up to a total of $1500 in credits can be claimed. A $30,000 or more in solar panels can help you save approximately $10,000 in taxes. There is carry over provision to future years.

10. Itemize or not ? Schedule A for 1040, helps save taxes for those who itemize. Even if you don't, another $1000 is available for non-itemizers.

11. Had a Second Job? To meet ends meet, or being part-time at primary job, those who had a second job can deduct, 0.55 cents per mile on travel to second job, as well as costs associated with a home office.

12. Moved, 50 miles plus? As in previous years, moving expenses are deductible, rental, supplies, meals etc can be included, for a taking up a new job.

13. High Earner? $2,433 is available as credit. the $3,650 exemptions lost to high earners now stops at $2,433, and is not zero. Higher deductions on itemizing are available to those

who make more than $166,000.

14. Pay into Deductible IRA, if you do not have pension plan at Work, or in your Business. Roth might be better in long term. The amounts to contribute have increased over the years to $5500 for each person, $6500 for those above 50 years of age.

15. Push more and more into your corporate pension plans (401-K, 403-b, defined benefit/contribution plans), and reduce your take home pay and save on taxes.

Remember, better late than never. In addition, every bit helps big in long term.

59

SECOND TO DIE

Selling whole life insurance has become increasingly difficult. The phrase "buy term and invest the difference" still attracts many people. The pitfalls of acquiring term insurance for long-term financial planning, however, are quite obvious. This is why the sale of variable life has increased so greatly, as people want a piece of the action from the stock market and mutual funds. Universal life often is sold because of its lower price and flexible premium when compared to whole life.

Survivorship life has been sold for its lower cost. It has lower mortality costs because the benefit is paid at the second death. It is popular for paying estate taxes at attractive rates. The aging of the population and its desire to pass billions of dollars to the next generation account for the increased use of this product. I believe huge amounts of this product will be placed in the coming decades.

For a survivorship life policy to function properly so that the death proceeds are not included in the estate, one has to buy it outside the estate, in a trust, or it must be owned by an heir. Many people buy survivorship policies for their lower costs, but fail to establish the irrevocable life insurance trust (ILIT) or other means to contain the proceeds outside their estate.

Survivorship life is sold as universal life, whole life, or variable life. In addition, a few companies offer survivorship life at low cost guaranteed renewable level term policy for a specific period, such as 20 or 25 years. The population's increased life-span has brought about some policies that are guaranteed until age 125.

At its core survivorship life is an estate planning tool used to pay estate taxes at nominal costs, transfer funds to the next generation, and minimize estate shrinkage.

I wish to examine two less-frequently discussed aspects of survivorship life policies. These are :
- Using it as a vehicle for cash accumulation, and
- Selling it as a permanent policy on two lives at a lower price and with a first-to-die rider.

Belonging to associations has attracted me for a long time. I belong to more then a dozen professional and social associations and attend their programs regularly.

Most of my prospects and clients come to me through hard work, cold calling, networking, and working with directories such as Indians in Atlanta, Physicians of Indian Origin, Asian Hotel Owners, and the like. I send newsletters to the entire memberships of these directories, and call those people with whom I am familiar with. Many people who move to town, start a new physician's practice, or open a hotel or other business call me for group or individual health insurance. After I have taken care of some of their insurance needs, I set up a meeting in their office or home to do financial planning.

I bring up estate shrinkage, life insurance, education, and retirement funding. Invariably, I hear the statements, "Buy term and invest the difference," and "Your money goes in a hole in whole life." Usually, I barely try to overcome these objections. I mention what the late Ben Feldman used to say: "Life insurance is such a complicated product, and so difficult to explain. If people knew what it could accomplish, they would stand in line to buy it, but it is so difficult to explain."

I try to explain that we are all mortals and one day will die because of old age, disease, or accident. "Kimascharyamatahparam" is an ancient Sanskrit saying from the Indian epic, Mahabharat, to which most of my Indian clients easily can relate. The expression means, "What is the greatest wonder?" The answer is that people are so fragile, and can die at any moment, but most act as if they are invincible.

I tell prospects that life insurance, which can be used for death benefit, cash value, retirement income, or all combined into one, can be purchased like an automobile. I use the examples of Mercedes Benz for $50,000, a Nissan Maxima for $25,000, or a Ford Escort for $12,000. All these cars come with several options – a sun roof, leather seats, cruise control, anti-lock brakes, etc. A person cannot, however, pay only a little and get a fancy, luxury car. I offer inexpensive term, like the Ford, universal life, like the Nissan, and whole life, which I tell prospects is like a Mercedes.

I find that many prospects lose their resistance when I tell them that I am an independent agent and won't push a product or company on them. I keep a few industry papers and comparisons handy to discuss prospects' concerns. Everyone has a list of best companies. Generally these lists are correct, but a specific product and specific need is met better by one company than the other.

I recommend two to three companies to prospects, explain each company's product, suggest a tentative premium amount, ask prospects to fill out an application, pick up a check, and leave an illustration or two. We agree that the prospects will go through a health examination soon, meet with me again after three or four weeks to examine the policy, and until then will have the option not to buy the plan and get a full refund. My prospects usually apply for whole life, but to be safe, I have them sign two illustrations, one on ten-year level term, the other on whole life. The whole life about which I am talking is survivorship life on two people. The prospects get four weeks to make a decision, while the insurance company is underwriting the case.

The advantages and virtues of a good brokerage manager or a general agent for a strong company who is available to make a prospect visit with the agent and push the case through underwriting never can be overemphasized. Luckily, I have a host of such support available in Atlanta, including the excellent office staffs of these people. Many of the people in these offices can run dazzling illustrations to fit any need, and can coordinate the whole process quite efficiently.

The first time I meet a prospect, we do not go through the entire process. At the first meeting, I spend an hour in fact finding. At the next meeting, a week later at my office, I have proposals and applications. Many times the health examination can be arranged during the interlude, so that underwriting will receive the application and medical records almost simultaneously.

Placing a survivorship policy is not always easy; 10% to 15% of cases do not get placed. About 10% to 15% of my prospects ask to be issued two separate level term policies, which most companies will do gladly. About 60% to 70% of the policies I place are permanent products.

The premiums I write generally are $12,000 to $24,000 a year or more. I always recommend automatic bank draft. Many times clients have looked on the Internet for the price or rating of companies, or have called toll-free quote services. I always honor client's wishes, but point out the differences between premiums and strength of companies. I always offer inexpensive term insurance, and hope for its conversion when clients have more cash.

I sell survivorship life. About 15% of my prospects do not buy or their policies are not placed after they are issued, and 15% buy only term. Those who have term or other forms of permanent insurance do not like to talk about estate or financial planning. Many of them also insist on an unlimited marital deduction, and do not like to think that both spouses might die in a common accident. If both did die, one shortly after the other, this might not leave enough time or insurability for the surviving spouse to plan for paying estate taxes through a survivorship policy outside of the estate or in a trust.

I recommend a survivorship policy with a first-to-die rider on both spouses (or business partners), with waiver of premium, additional term insurance, and accidental death riders. I recommend whole life for more money, universal life for less to begin with and to retain flexibility to dump in funds in the future to generate tax-deferred cash, and variable life to participate in the equity market. These are richly designed policies with high face values, in most cases one to five million dollars. These policies cover both spouses or partners. The waiver of premium rider takes care of the premium payment in the case of total disability. Clients will receive twice the coverage in the case of accidental death. And the additional term rider can be converted to a permanent form of insurance later, and will provide plenty of discretionary cash.

Survivorship life is insurance on two persons, at a lower cost because of lower mortality charges. Adding a first-to-die rider can make this policy as effective as having two separate policies, which may be separated (like a joint life protector) at divorce, dissolution of partnership, or for other reasons. Lower insurance costs generate more cash that can be used for retirement income.

Many clients have bought these plans because they find so many features they want in one policy: a flexible premium payment, the option of dropping unnecessary coverage in the future, and the options of using it for income at retirement or for education funding, not simply for paying estate taxes.

60

Social In(Security)

Will social security play a bigger role for retirement benefits of baby boomers and others in coming years or will it go bust, as it was aptly called, social (in)security sometimes ago?

The current economic turmoil, loss of wealth and pension funds makes more people to look forward towards secured benefits. Forecasting the future of social security, is complicated, but the following facts will help those who still depend on the Government for their welfare, and do not believe that the Government is 'necessary evil', like most of the super-rich do.

Q. Where does one find answers to questions about social security benefits ?

A. The Social Security Administration Office in your area, Social Security web site : www.socialsecurity.gov. Phone : 1-800-772-1213. Booklet, 2016 Guide to Social Security, 44th Edition, (publisher : Mercer, Louisville, KY) by Doma Clements, is well written and very informative.

Q. When should one file for Social Security Benefits ?

A. Normally three month before one qualifies for Benefits, in person, at the social security office, with : social security card, proof of age, tax-return of previous year and one or more of the documents related to marriage, divorce and death.

Q. What is the maximum retirement benefit can one receive from social security administration ?

A. $2,232 at age 65, based on earnings and amounts contributted to the account during working years. There is always an inflation factor built in the system, that increases the benefits over the years. This is called social security cost of living adjustment (COLA), generally a 4% increase per year.

Q. How do I get an estimate of my future benefits or earnings ?

A. Social Security Administration regularly sends statements to those who qualify to receive benefits. One can also request, 'Personal Earnings and Benefit Estimate Statement' from the Administration.

Q. When do I receive my Benefits ?

A. Benefits can be received earliest at age 62. But the full benefits (100%) is generally available at age 65. Benefits at earlier ages, like 62, are reduced by 25% of the total benefits available at full retirement. Full retirement age, or availability of 100% of benefits is determined by the year one was born in, as explained below :

Year of birth, 1937, full retirement age 65. Born between 1938-1942, changes to 66.

After 1955, 66 years and few months. Born 1960 and later, the full retirement age is 67.

Congress has not decided, what it will do for people who are even younger.

Q. Can I receive benefits at 62, if I am still working ?

A. May be, Provided your earnings are not much, say $12,000 a year or less.

It is same for people who are self-employed.

Q. Are social security benefits taxed by IRS ?

A. Again, may be, People making $24,000 a year or less, in-cluding social security benefits (and any spousal income in case of joint returns, may receive the benefits tax-free. Those making above $24,000 through $44,000, may have to pay income taxes on 50% of the social security earnings. For those earning more than $44,000, about 80% of the benefits should be taxed. Further details are mentioned in IRS publications : 554 (Tax Information for Older Americans), and 915 (Social Security Benefits). IRS can be reached at : http://www.irs.gov or 1-800-829-3676.

Q. How can i reduce my Social Security taxes during working years, and increase my benefits in retirement ?

A. There are legitimate ways allowed by Social Security Administration, IRS (Internal Revenue Service, and DOL (Department of Labor) to accomplish this. These organizations really encourage workers and retirees by placing funds in several plans to reduce their tax liability. A competent accountant, tax- and elder-law attomey, and a financial planner can help design such plans and programs.

Q. What other benefits does Social Security Administration provide, in addition to retirement benefits ?

A. There are several, but three of them stand out. Disability Benefits, Survivor Benefits and Medicare. All three of them need detailed and seperate treatments.

61

Survivorship Life

We obtain a list from various sources of affluent members of the community such as physicians, business owners, and retired persons with large pension funds. Prospects with whom I already have met are easier to reach on the telephone.

Sending a prospecting letter explaining the need for estate planning, is important. The letter could be two paragraphs, with a quotation from a famous person about the difficulty of maintaining wealth as the first paragraph.

I follow the quote with a concept stated in three to five lines, like estate exclusion, early retirement with unlimited tax-free benefits, or the estate taxation rate for a $5 million estate.

Changes in 1993 to OBRA, the Omnibus Budget Reconciliation Act of 1987, reduced the maximum compensation that can be counted for qualified retirement plan purposes to $150,000, down from $253,840. To discuss the solutions to estate and retirement planning problems. "Non-U.S. citizens need establish revocable living, irrevocable insurance, charitable remainder, qualified domestic, or other kinds of trusts before it is too late."

I need to make repeated and persistent calls to succeed in getting appointments. Getting high-quality appointments is difficult and takes time.

A thorough fact finding should cover my prospect's earnings, savings, expenses, and insurance policies and investments, which include automobile, home, business, professional liability, disability, health, dental, and life insurance, as well as contributions to pension plans, college funding for children, retirement plans, and charitable contributions. It is imperative that the agent knows the full picture to plan the prospect's estate.

We try to establish the estate's value. Net worth is important, which includes all debts, such as unpaid home mortgages and business loans, and obligations to establish a huge dollar amount that we need to protect.

If both spouses die in a common accident, the policy proceeds on their lives will be included in their estate unless they have established an insurance trust. Thus, need for enough funds to pay estate taxes, liquidate debts, meet planned family and personal obligations, help fund charities, and care for his or her dreams and aspirations is established. Projections on the growth in the estate's value over time. My prospect and I discuss shrinkage possibilities in the estate's value from taxes, inflation, and other factors.

Contacting prospect's accountant, attorney, or both, to discuss the estate planning matters from their viewpoint is important.

We explore the need for a living or irrevocable trust and a survivorship life insurance policy, sometimes with a first-to-die rider to eliminate the small, inexpensive term insurance policies. I do not try to replace or count the existing policies, as they are meant for a surviving spouse, children, or charity. Depending on the cash flow, I determine the premium and waiver.

We run illustrations, proposals, or both, preferably from more than one company and of more than one kind of policy, that is, a mix of whole life and term insurance riders. For clients that are close to their fifties. I recommend they pay enough funds into the policy so that they can achieve a projected vanish year of age 64. This creates plenty of cash at retirement. If life insurance and estate tax needs decrease, one can take part of the survivorship life policy's cash value as a loan, which may reduce the policy's face value.

Several premium variations help the client choose a level with which he or she is comfortable. In my experience, practically everyone likes to pay the lowest premium amount. When I show the availability of cash for distribution many clients opt for higher premiums.

My client signs the policy applications and related documents, and I submit the papers for underwriting to the carrier on which my client and I mutually have agreed.

I follow through by working with paramedicals, chest X-ray technicians, and physicians to schedule and complete all necessary requirements, including the attending physician's statement (APS). I also collect financial documents from the accountant and any existing trust information from the attorneys during this phase. More telephone calls and a few more visits to the accountant and the prospect are needed to complete the underwriting process.

A good rapport with the insurer's local brokerage officer is critical to ensure the policy's smooth issue. Dealing with the competition and building trust with prospects is all the more necessary for the agent at this point.

After the company issues the policy, I visit with the accountant and discuss the numbers, premiums, and projected cash values. My experience is that accountants are conservative and do not like to look at anything above 6% interest. The accountant's help is critical in placing the policy and collecting the premium.

Obtaining annual premiums has been difficult for me, so I settle for the monthly automatic bank draft mode of premium payment. Before the policy is dated, my prospect, his or her advisers, and I determine the prospect's need for a trust or whether to name a heir as the policy owner.

Clients many times are more comfortable with one carrier than another carrier because of advertising or word of mouth. I respect their choice if the insurer is a high-quality company.

Placing the policy and getting paid for my work does not complete the task. We invite him or her for a lunch meeting to discuss any other concerns he or she might have. The discussion opens possibilities of further business and referrals.

Cases that do not move forward all the way also generate some ancillary and small business, such as group health insurance, casualty insurance, and liability insurance cases that I place with colleagues who specialize in the specific areas. Many times a senior colleague, especially with a CPA designation, JD designation, or both, helps to manage complicated cases and shares in compensation.

My sales process is time-consuming and arduous, but the rewards and enjoyment make it worth the effort. I find it satisfying to help an affluent person plan his or her estate well, in addition to being adequately compensated for the effort.

62

Tax Efficiency

Numerous things need to be done before 12-31, to save on taxes, which have been going up and up for the last few years. 46% of what you make could go in income taxes, 39.6% for Federal, and 6% for State.

In addition, sales-, property-, medicare-, FICA-, social security- and other-taxes one pays, brings the net income below 50% of the gross. Uncle Sam collects over 50% of your earnings, like you work for the Government and the Tax Collecting Authorities.

Hence several measures are available to minimize the tax burden, and most need to be done before the end of the year:

1. Maximize your retirement contributions, which is 'pay yourself first'. Push $18,000 into a 401(K) plan at Work. IRA can accommodate, up to $6500. SEP can take up to $52,000. But Defined Benefit Plans accept up to $210,000 pre-tax.

2. If the Goddess of Stock market was kind to you this year, take your losses, by selling bad investments And offset the realized gains.

3. Give gifts, to reduce gift and estate taxes. $14,000 can be given by each spouse, for a total of $28,000 to as many people as you choose, especially to children and grand children.

4. When you earn money, uncle Sam takes 45% in taxes, when you die, he takes 55%. Seems unfair ? It is. But there are ways to avoid those high taxes, if one can set up wills and trusts properly.

5. Being 71 years old, one has to face the RMD, required minimum distribution, to avoid tax penalties, if there be huge assets inside a pension/retirement plan. But there are several tax-efficient investment to minimize the erosion of assets. Being less than 60, also triggers penalties if one tries to tap into retirement accounts. There are ways to minimize or avoid those taxes and fines.

6. Keep your investments on track, and re-balance portfolios, for profit and efficiency. A proper mixture of various asset classes will provide growth, and will help avoid sudden downfall in the market. No risk no gain, is true, but how much risk is desirable, and what gain and losses one can manage over a fixed period of time, is generally illusive, and requires expert advise.

7. Charities are of great help. They reduce taxes, and can be set up to help the donor to receive funds later in tax-efficient ways, and create a legacy. Be charitable. Make yourself the beneficiary of the charity.

63

Tax-deductible Life Insurance

We tend not to use premiums for life insurance, as a tax-deductible item, since the benefits will become taxable. 'Pennywise, but Pound foolish' will describe this situation. You buy a term life policy of $1 Million, pay a premium of $100/ month or $1200/year. If you treat the premium as tax-deductible expense, and save $100 - $300 in taxes, your beneficiary may have to pay $300,000 - $500,000 in taxes form the death benefit proceeds, of $1 Million. Hence life insurance is always purchased with after-tax dollars.

However, there are ways to buy life insurance, deduct the premium as tax-deductible item, and buy with Pre-tax dollars, like a business expense, or like IRA and other retirement plan. In this situation the premiums are tax deductible, and the proceeds of life insurance, the death benefit to the beneficiary, are still tax-free.

Life insurance in such cases is made part of a qualified retirement plan, where premiums are tax-deducted, Premature death benefits, are paid to the beneficiary or insured, tax-free. A small business owner can offer this golden handcuff, to employees, saying if you stay with the company for a certain number of years, we will have life insurance, in case of death for the family, income protection for the employee in case of prolonged sickness, and eventually retirement benefits, after 65 or so. All the premiums paid are tax-deductible to the business, and the business controls how the proceeds will be provided to the heirs of an employee, or to the employees directly.

Internal Revenue Service, IRS and DOL, Department of Labor have well defined, elaborate and complicated rules to establish and manage these plans for the benefit of all concerned. In such plans, one can put huge sums of funds on a tax deductible basis, not limited like IRA for $5500-$6500, or 401(K) For $18,000, but up to $210,000, all on tax deductible basis.

Here is an example, to explain the situation. One spends 18 years in high school, 4 years in college, another 4 years in medical school, 3-4 years in residency, and then another 7 years to become a specialist, cardiologist, surgeon, neurologist etc. By the time a well trained doctor starts practicing, he/she is already 37- 39 - 41 years old, and earns $300K to $900K or more a year. This person has just 20 years to retire, and can put $5000 a year or so in an IRA, for the next 20 years, which will not generate enough funds to maintain his/her life style, in retirement. Hence the provision, of putting $210K a year, into defined benefit plan, where $10,000 to $20,000 can be taken as pension, every month from age 62, 65, through age 85,90, and also leave Millions of Dollars for spouse and children, as life insurance.

Not only physicians, but any business owner is allowed to put $50,000 to $200,000 per year into the pension trust, with 100% tax-deductible dollars, and can also have tax-deductible life insurance in the same plan.

This has been one of the most efficient ways to create wealth, for one's own benefit and for the posterity.

Timely Thought

Supreme Court Justice Brandeis, said the following :

" I live in Alexandria Virginia. Near the Supreme Court Chambers is a toll bridge across the Potomac.

When in a rush, I pay the dollar toll and get home early. However, I usually drive outside the downtown section of the city and cross the Potomac on a free bridge.

This bridge was placed outside the downtown Washington D.C. area to serve a useful social service, getting drivers to drive the extra mile to alleviate congestion during the rush hour.

If I went through the toll bridge and through the barrier without paying the toll, I would be committing Tax Evasion !

If, however, I drive the extra mile and drive outside the city of Washington to the free bridge, I am using a legitimate, logical and suitable method of tax avoidance, and I am performing a useful social service by doing so.

For my Tax Evasion, I should be punished. For my Tax Avoidance, I should be commended.

The tragedy of life today is that so few people know that the free bridge exists."

It is time to file tax returns. There are several methods of saving on taxes. Most of them are related to pension and retirement benefits, like IRA, SEP, Defined Benefit-, Profit Sharing-, Simple, 401(K), 403(b), 412(e).....Plans. Not enough people are aware of these plans, and most never take advantage of these IRS and DOL approved plans, available for individuals and corporations.

TRUIRJCA

Truirjca is not from Sanskrit. But acronym for, Tax Relief, Unemployment Insurance Reauthorization and Job Creation Act of 2010.

For simplification, it is referred as Tax Relief Act of 2010 (TRA 2010). In the last days of 2010 Congress passed this tax law, with help from President Obama, with the longest and most tongue-twisting name. It simply means extension of 'Bush Tax Cuts' for two years, until December 31, 2012.

Years 2011 and 2012, were very busy for Estate Planners, since all existing Estate Plans, Wills and Trusts should be reviewed for TRA 2010.

President Bush in 2001 helped create, EGTRRA, Economic Growth and Tax Relief Reconciliation Act, which has been modified into TRA 2010.

All existing Estate Plans should be reviewed and updated. The States have enacted their own estate taxes due to the reduction of estate taxes at Federal level. Beginning Jan 1, 2017, estate tax rules will change again, They are now at $5.4 Million and 40%, whosoever enters the White House, lifetime gifting options will change.

It may be prudent to anticipate future changes, though it is difficult to predict what Congress will do, and prepare for the inevitable. Federal Estate Tax exemptions are expected to revert to $1 Million, and the estate tax rate to a maximum of 55%.

This should also affect, Defined Benefit Plans, Retirement Planning and Business Succession. Tools for implementing the new paradigms need, thus, to be visited every year. It is not good to get shocked and surprised in 2017.

Universal Life

As the name suggests, universal life insurance (UL) should be the product of universal appeal and use. For a period I sold only whole life or term policies if someone wanted inexpensive or temporary insurance. Many of my colleagues held a similar view. They believed the lack of built-in guarantees made UL less appealing than whole life. If it were necessary to lower premiums, they would prefer to mix term and whole life than use universal life.

We sold term policies thinking that many would convert to whole life when the premium rose or when insurability was at risk. UL was used as something less desirable than whole life. Many top-ranked insurers did not provide a UL product. Gradually, confidence in UL's utility enabled many more companies to offer it.

To simplify the difference for my prospects, I compare buying insurance to buying a car — buying term is like getting a Ford Escort, buying UL is like getting a Honda Accord, and whole life is like purchasing a Mercedes Benz. I compare accidental death, waiver of premium, and spouse and children riders to extras like leather interior, sunroof, and anti-lock brakes.

Most of my prospects purchase term insurance. I do not object, but instead encourage them to get what makes them comfortable. I always point out what is best for them based on their financial situation and insurance needs. Eventually, many who buy term will convert to permanent insurance. I offer both UL and whole life. UL usually is the better solution, as the premium differences aren't that great and policyholders can dump in funds whenever they like.

Many companies that started business with the slogan "buy term and invest the difference" have seen most followers flying into different camps. Now they use the motto "buy insurance as a shell, put stocks around it, and enjoy tax-deferred growth of your mutual funds." These companies operate like brain-surgeons –they are specialized and offer only one product. They offer 20-year level term plus lousy mutual funds, or variable life with high asset charge mutual funds. Many of these companies are successful, but incorrect in selling the same plan to all.

I operate as a general practitioner who sells automobile, home, individual, group, and health insurance, as well as Section 401(k) plans and other pension products, all kinds of life and disability insurance, and investment vehicles.

UL is growing bigger in my portfolio for the following reasons:

Term insurance is temporary, pure insurance, no money back unless the policyholder purchases a participating policy that will charge a higher premium and return dividends.

No one, it seems, wants to buy whole life. This is unfortunate. But insurance producer associations do not address the issue. The late Ben Feldman best described whole life when he said, "If people knew what this product can do they would flock to buy it, but it is so difficult to explain it to the general public."

Success in selling whole life depends on how well the producer can explain it. The whole life market, however, has been slipping because of the stock market's phenomenal success. It also is affected by these policies' high premium structures, which offer so many guarantees and generate so much cash value in the product.

Term is like renting. Whole life is like buying and generating equities so that one can pay it off one day. UL is more versatile as it offers a lease-purchase arrangement. The client can pay low, not worry about cash value, invest elsewhere, and have

(159)

low premium. This could be structured as a term policy. With definite or indefinite (to age 121) numbers of premiums to be paid. There is plenty of scope for creating a side fund or annuity, at guaranteed/market rate of interest to generate cash, or to vanish the premium at a desirable time. Numerous points, however, must be explained to prospects and clients, such as mortality charges, insurance cost, premium tax, dividend generated, and so on.

In variable life, several new parameters enter the picture, including all of the ramifications of managing mutual funds — asset charges, expenses of buying and selling stock, and paying and deferring taxes in the sub-accounts. Increased complications and flexibility make it a more advanced machine or product, but the chances of malfunction also are increased.

UL should be able to solve more problems than whole or term alone because of its premium flexibility and potential of higher returns resulting from market conditions. The trend of not having dividends should be of little concern, as mutual companies are disappearing one after another and are being replaced by stock companies. Lately, mutual companies had a come back and stock companies lost their high ratings.

In the late 1970s when interest rates were 19% and whole life was paying 6%, people borrowed cash value to put in certificates of deposit and bank investments. The demise of many insurance companies was one of these reasons. Most companies illustrated a high interest rate and vanishing premium proposals, which still haunt them in court cases.

This dichotomy of principle and practice is one reason producers are losing and getting out of the business. This also makes recruiting new producers difficult.

People know they are not dying anytime soon and they do not want to plan for death. About 60% of marriages evaporate into divorce, so why buy life insurance? Insurance companies are dropping the sacred word "life" from their names and calling themselves financial companies, which makes sense as selling life insurance becomes more difficult and stigmatized. I wish people received citations for not having life, health, and disability insurance as they do for lack of auto insurance.

Interest-sensitive traditional and variable life products were introduced to sell life insurance with sizzle, to prey on prospects' greed. The stock market's lessons in the past months should give some reason not to expect life insurance to perform as an investment vehicle, but a conservative place to save funds for retirement or other purposes in addition to life insurance.

A select group of companies offer life policies through the investment of side funds in the S&P 500 index. I have sold these to clients who do not want the risk of variable life and wanted to settle for more modest gains, but less risk. I, however, find these policies less attractive than the S&P 500 index annuities, where the gains made in one cycle are preserved when the index slips down. The index UL has not shown much higher returns compared to traditional UL. The S&P 500 Index UL, however, can be expected to keep a balance between high-risk variable life and low-return traditional universal life, and the low-return whole life.

Instead of selling two term policies, for general use or for such a specialized use, like stock redemption in a buy-sell agreement, I can design a second-to-die policy for two or more business partners, or spouses, or family members, with a first-to-die rider. This can include multiple lives, accidental death enhancements, waiver of premium, and other features. By dumping in higher amounts of cash, vanishing premiums can be achieved or it can be made to act as retirement vehicle, to generate a steady income source in later years. Both traditional and variable universal life policies may be put to such uses.

But, When stock market is loosing ground. The dividends in universal life product can accommodate numerous needs from untimely death, level low premiums for a certain number of years, college funding, to retirement.

Term insurance is cheap and does not last long. Term policies get dropped by clients and often are converted into permanent products and annuities become very attractive.

UL is a better answer to a need for low premiums, long-time coverage, ability to add extra funds, the addition of many desirable features, and the deletion of unwanted features.

Many kinds of people make great UL prospects. Single adults can use UL to pay for last expenses, have a guaranteed future insurability at a relatively lower cost, and for savings and retirement benefits in future.

Single parents can use the product to accumulate cash for college education, keep death benefits for immediate or future needs at low costs, and switch to a savings mode, higher premium in the policy after they become empty nesters.

Two-income families also can obtain death benefits, college funding, and retirement savings all in one policy at affordable premiums rates and flexible patterns. Waiver of premium and accidental death can enhance the coverage. The policy offers them a way to accumulate cash for dependents, partners, and themselves at attractive rates of return, without much risk and at tax-deferred basis.

UL also is a good policy for juveniles. In addition to putting funds in the stock market for college funding, parents should have a UL policy on each child to ensure future insurability. I recommend paying high enough premiums that the policy will pay for itself after 10 years. I also recommend adding death benefit option 2 to increase the benefits on a regular basis, so that one policy on a child can last for his or her lifetime.

Yes/No, Life Insurance

Is insurance a necessary evil ? With so many kinds, we need to acquire, car, home, biz, liability, medical, dental, vision, disability, long term care, life, malpractice etc, it may seem so. But that is not true. Insurance is a social device, where members put a small portion of their funds in a common pool, called premium, and expect to get a bigger amount paid, called claim at time of loss. Insurance companies that collect premiums and pay claims are allowed to keep only 2% of the premiums collected for their administrative functions, hence they have to raise premiums so often. Most often the profits are returned back to the public as dividends, which is normally return of premium, and non-taxable.

The most dreaded is life insurance, which no one wants to buy. But here are some data, contrary to popular belief. Which industry the people do not want to work for as salespeople ? Insurance. Which industry has the largest number of sales people? The answer again is Insurance. Which product people least want to buy ? Answer, insurance. Which product is sold most ? Again, Insurance. Which kind of sales people make the highest income ? The insurance Agents, especially the life insurance agents.

Why then people are not buying life insurance ?

They do not have NEED for it. Life insurance has to be purchased when you do not need it. When you need,you can not get it. People do not Want to spend MONEY to buy it. Life Insurance is bought with good health and is paid for by money, premium. It is necessary evil, 8-10% of gross income must be spent to buy insurance, to protect economic losses. People are not in HURRY to buy insurance. But they have to be in hurry. Your health can change overnight, you can get killed or disabled in an accident, anytime. Procrastination and not being prudent creates biggest of disasters.

Buy as much life insurance as you can, inflation will erode its value over time, and you may not qualify to get more at a lower rate in future. Just hurry to place it in force. Term insurance, temporary, the cheap stuff, is the most expensive way to buy insurance, 97% get cancelled and never Pay claims. Permanent is expensive, but 100% result into claims, and those cost lots of funds to the insurance company, much more than they charge in premiums. Who are the biggest life insurance purchasers ? The Banks. They bring millions and billions of dollar to insurance companies to buy whole life insurance. They get 6-7% tax-deferred dividends, tax-free death benefits at pennies for dollars. Insurance companies always avoid issuing those big policies for banks, not taking too much risk, and be liquid for the small policy owners.

Appendix

BLIND MEN AND ELEPHANT

The story, elephant examined by six blind men, or in dark, originated in India, may be in Panchtantra, which has numerous animal fables, narrated by Pandit Visnu Sarma, for the education of the sons of a King.

Examining an elephant by blind men, has eventually diffused into various faiths : Hinduism, Jain, Buddhist, Sufi, Bahai etc. The lore became known to the West, when American Poet John Godfrey Saxe (in the 18th Century) wrote a poem on this subject. This poem was included in the English Text Book, in High School, which I read in 1955, in Bihar (Mithila), India, and has stayed in my memory since then.

The poem is available and recited on You Tube. Brooklyn Museum has a painting, 'The Blind Men Appraising an Elephant' by Ohara Donshu from the early 19th Century. There is also a famous Wall Mural, on this concept, in Thailand. Wikipedia has also described this situation, which includes the painting from the Brooklyn Museum as well as the Wall Mural from Thailand. The number of men, examining the elephant vary from three to six. But they convey the same concept of one-sided knowledge, and lack of holistic, complete and comprehensive view about the matters of importance.

A group of blind men (or men in dark) touch an elephant to learn, what it is like. Each feels a different, but only one part of the elephant. They are in complete disagreement, saying elephant is like a snake (tail), a brush (end of tail), pillar (legs), wall (sides), fan (ears), spear(tusks), etc. No one can see the whole picture, which has important religious and cultural implications, where different faiths argue on their uniqueness, but a holistic view comes only from a man with sight, who sees the whole elephant from a distance, in light, and describes it properly. He/She also explains the debating men, that they are blind, and have a single, narrow, specialized view of the subject.

Hence Lord Ganesha, with his Elephant Head is considered so wise. No wonder, the Mouse of Ganeshji has evolved into the tool (Mouse) of Information Technology.

Reference to this fact appears in Bible (Luke, Matthews), Kathopanishad, Buddhist Sukta, as well as, in Greek, Latin, Arabic and Russian translations.

This also leads to the Metaphor, if the 'Blind leads the Blind', it will result in both falling into a pit, which has been said again and again since antiquity. One has to get out of ignorance and have a holistic picture of any situation, is the moral of the story.

Based on this theme, 'Invest & Insure' Discusses the financial and investment advise we often receive from various professionals, like attorney, accountant, realtor, lender, builder, insurance agent, and others about any matter, who provide us their view point and implement their recommendations, which is generally incomplete and one sided. A comprehensive apporach to any financial problem, will thus be available only from a competent 'Financial Planner' who operates like a 'family physicain' and not like a 'neurosurgeon'. In this age of 'specialization', where a 'generalist', receives less respect and lower fees, compared to a 'specialist', needs to be revisited.

There are two books, 'The Blind Men and The Elephant', from Scholastic by Backstein/Mitra for children, and the same title, by Schmaltz, from BK on Project Management.

Invest and Insure

Elephant and Six Blind men.

The famous parable of explaining the partial, individual, and holistic views of situations in life.

Elephant is like the trunk of a tree, said the first man, touching the feet. It is like a rope, second blind man was holding the tail in his hand.

The third said, it is like a wall, experiencing the big flat body, the sides. The fourth, said it is like a huge fan, touching the ear.

Said the fifth, it is like spears, touching the tusks. The sixth person said, it is like a brush, from the end of the tail.

Most specialists will do the same. We must have a holistic view of things, not understanding things from a single narrow perspective.

In investment, insurance, money management, and risk assessment, the views of an attorney, architect, accountant, realtor, lender, stock broker, insurance agent, friend, a smart family member and others, like financial gurus on TV, magazines, and in Press, who always give you tips, probably act like one of those blind men, understanding just one aspect of any situation.

Their advice should be integrated by a qualified Financial Planner, into one holistic view of the matter, analyzed in detail, then determine solutions and finally provide recommendations for the financial well being of individuals, businesses and institutions for a long time, that may last generations.

Implementing those recommendations, and setting up accounts for the smooth functioning of the financial growth, and obtaining predictable and desirable results, requires expertise, and costs money.

There are no short cuts, and plenty of time, effort and funds are required, to succeed.

FATCA, foreign account tax compliance act, Swiss and Panama Bank accounts, and other Tax Havens are being pursued with great vigor, by Governments all over the world, especially related to Money Laundering.

Continued from Back......

The third approached the animal, and, happening to take,
the squirming trunk within his hands,
"I see", quothe he, " the elephant is very like a SNAKE !"

The fourth reached out an eager hand And felt about the knee
'What most this wondrous beast is like, is mighty plain,'
'Tis clear enough the elephant is very like a TREE !"

The fifth, who chanced to touch the ear, Said; 'E'en the blindest man
can tell what this resembles most; Deny the fact who can,
This marvel of an elephant, is very like a FAN !"

The sixth no sooner had begun, about the beast to grope,
than, seizing on the swinging tail, that fell within his scope,
'I see,' quothe he, 'the elephant is very like a ROPE !"

And so these men of Indostan, disputed loud and long,
each in his own opinion, exceeding stiff and strong,
Though each was partly in the right, and all were in the wrong!

So, oft in theologic wars, the disputants, I ween,
tread on in utter ignorance, of what each other mean,
and prate about the elephant, not one of them has seen!